ANDREW PE

A CRASH COURSE IN
ARTIFICIAL
INTELLIGENCE

What You Need to Know About the
Technology that will Change Everything

•

POINSSOT PRESS

DEDICATION

This is for my boys
—and their future

CONTENTS

CONTENTS

INTRODUCTION

A few years back, I found myself staring at my computer screen with a curious mix of skepticism and intrigue. I had just heard about ChatGPT, an AI tool that promised to revolutionize how we interact with machines. As an author who cherishes writing, I was naturally apprehensive. *Could this newfangled algorithm really do what I do? Or worse: Will it steal my job?*

Curiosity got the better of me, and I decided to give it a whirl. To say I was amazed would be an understatement. The AI didn't just spit out words; it crafted coherent ideas, offering insights I hadn't considered. What began as an experiment soon evolved into a daily tool. It transformed my writing process, boosting my creativity and efficiency. My initial fear of AI taking over my job turned into excitement about the untold possibilities it could bring.

Artificial Intelligence is not just a tech buzzword. It's a force reshaping industry, from healthcare to entertainment. It's also affecting our everyday lives in ways we might not fully grasp. Did you know that AI is projected to contribute over $15 trillion to the global economy by 2030? That's more than the GDP of China and India combined, which is why it's crucial for us to understand this technology—because, like it or not, it's here to stay.

This book will be your guide through the fascinating world of Artificial Intelligence. It's not just about understanding algorithms or data. It's about the stories and histories that make AI what it is today. We'll explore practical insights that can help demystify AI and show you how to use it for your benefit. The aim is to make AI less intimidating and more of a friendly tool you can rely on.

After I got over my initial reticence about AI, I realized it wasn't about replacement. It was about enhancement. AI became my collaborator, pushing my boundaries and allowing me to explore new creative territories. This book reflects that transformation. It's a journey I want to take you on, showing how embracing AI can lead to unexpected and rewarding results.

This is a primer for people who are curious about what AI will mean in our lives. Whether you're worried about job security or excited about new tech possibilities, this book has something for you. You may have questions or even misconceptions about AI. We will address those head-on, providing clear answers and insights.

The chapters are structured to take you on a journey. We start with the history of AI and travel through its current applications, \examining ethical considerations. We'll also gaze into the future, imagining what AI could become. Each section has engaging content designed to keep you informed and entertained.

I encourage you to actively engage with the material. Think critically about how AI fits into your life. Reflect on how you can adapt to this new reality and leverage AI for personal and professional growth. Check out the Resources Appendix, which gives you a list of tools you can start using right now. By the end, you should have a clearer picture of what AI can do and how it can be your ally.

The key takeaway here is simple: AI is a transformative force. Understanding it is not just beneficial; it's necessary. I hope this book captivates your interest and provides a roadmap for navigating this game-changing technology. Feel free at any point to jump in and use these resources at the end of the book to see for yourself the mind-boggling capabilities of this wild and new frontier known as Artificial Intelligence.

THE BASICS

I found myself in a spirited debate with a close friend, a tech enthusiast who couldn't stop talking about artificial intelligence. At the time, my knowledge of AI was limited to sci-fi movies, where robots often went rogue. As our discussion progressed, he challenged me with a simple question: "Do you realize that every time you ask Siri for the weather, you're engaging with AI?" *What a revelation!* I suddenly realized I had already been interacting with AI almost daily, completely unaware of its pervasive presence in my life. This conversation sparked my curiosity and set me on a path to unravel the mysteries of this new and powerful technology.

At its core, AI is the simulation of human intelligence processes by machines, particularly computer systems. This might sound a bit abstract but think of it this way: AI involves tasks that require human-like decision-making capabilities. So, it's about teaching computers to think, learn, and problem-solve in ways that mimic human cognition. When you hear AI, imagine a virtual brain that can sift through vast amounts of data, recognize patterns, and make decisions based on that analysis. This capability gives AI the capability of driving advancements in fields ranging from medicine to finance. But it's not just about crunching numbers; it's about enabling machines to perform tasks that once seemed exclusively human.

Diving deeper, AI comprises several core components that work in tandem to achieve these remarkable feats. Learning is at the heart of AI. This involves algorithms that allow systems to improve over time by recognizing patterns and making data-driven predictions. Reasoning enables AI to make sense of complex information, drawing logical conclusions, much like we do when solving puzzles. Then there's problem-solving, which involves the ability to tackle challenges and identify the most effective solutions. Perception and language understanding are equally vital, allowing AI to interpret visual data and comprehend human language, bridging the gap between humans and machines. Each component plays a crucial role, working together to create systems that are both versatile and adaptable.

Despite its impressive capabilities, AI is often misunderstood. A common misconception is that AI is synonymous with robots, but that's not entirely accurate. While robots can be equipped with AI, the technology itself is a broad field encompassing software that runs on various platforms, from smartphones to data centers. Another myth is that AI possesses consciousness or emotions. In reality, AI is a collection of algorithms lacking awareness; it doesn't feel joy or sadness. It processes data according to programmed rules, making it a tool—albeit a sophisticated one—designed to assist and augment human abilities.

AI is subtly woven into the fabric of our daily lives, sometimes without us even noticing. Consider smart assistants like Alexa and Siri, which have become household fixtures. These AI-driven devices use speech recognition to respond to commands, making everyday tasks more convenient. Then there are recommendation systems on platforms like Netflix and Amazon. These systems analyze your preferences and viewing habits to suggest content tailored specifically to you. It's AI in action, helping you navigate the overwhelming array of choices in the digital world. These examples highlight how AI enhances our lives, offering convenience and personalization with a simple voice command or click of a button.

Reflection: Where's the AI in Your Life?

Consider how AI is present in your own life. Jot down instances where you've interacted with AI, whether it's through using a voice assistant, encountering targeted ads, or relying on navigation apps. Reflect on how these technologies have influenced your routines and decision-making processes. This exercise will help you appreciate the pervasive nature of AI and its role in shaping modern life.

Machine Learning vs. Deep Learning

Machine learning, a term that has steadily entered the lexicon of modern technology, is essentially about teaching computers to learn from experience. Imagine it as a classroom where computers attend daily lessons, absorbing information and refining their understanding over time. At its core, machine learning consists of algorithms that empower computers to make data-driven decisions. These algorithms sift through data, identify patterns, and make predictions or decisions without explicit programming for those tasks. Consider an email spam filter, a tool many of us use daily. It learns to differentiate between spam and legitimate emails by analyzing vast amounts of data, continually improving its accuracy based on user interactions. Each time you mark an email as spam, the system learns a little more about what spam looks like to you. It's this iterative learning process, fueled by data, that defines machine learning's essence.

Deep learning, on the other hand, takes the concept of machine learning and adds a new layer of complexity—several layers, in fact. Deep learning relies on neural networks, which are structures inspired by the human brain, to process information. These networks contain multiple layers that allow them to handle vast amounts of data and perform more intricate tasks. Think of deep learning as a multi-layered cake, where each layer adds depth and complexity to the flavor. Unlike traditional machine learning, which might focus on simpler tasks, deep learning excels in situations requiring intense data processing and pattern recognition. A prime example is image recognition systems, which can identify objects within pictures with remarkable precision. These systems analyze images pixel by pixel, learning to recognize shapes, colors, and textures in ways that mimic human visual perception. It's this capacity for handling complexity that sets deep learning apart from its machine learning counterpart.

Real-world applications of machine learning and deep learning are everywhere, often in places we least expect. In healthcare, machine learning algorithms assist doctors by analyzing medical records and suggesting potential diagnoses. They offer a second opinion; one backed by data and statistical analysis. Meanwhile, deep learning plays a pivotal role in autonomous vehicle navigation. These systems must process immense amounts of sensor data in real-time to make split-second decisions on the road, such as recognizing pedestrians and traffic signs. Voice recognition and natural language processing are other areas where deep learning shines. By dissecting the intricacies of human speech, systems like virtual assistants can understand and respond to spoken commands, translating our words into actions. The difference between the two lies in the complexity of the tasks they handle, with deep learning tackling the more intricate challenges thanks to its layered approach.

Case Study - Healthcare Diagnostics

In healthcare, the distinction between machine learning and deep learning becomes strikingly apparent. Machine learning models are adept at analyzing patient data, identifying trends, and predicting outcomes based on historical records. For instance, a machine learning algorithm might analyze a decade's worth of patient data to predict the likelihood of a disease's occurrence. Deep learning, however, goes a step further. Consider a deep learning model trained to analyze medical images, such as X-rays or MRIs. This model can identify anomalies, such as tumors, with a level of detail and accuracy that rivals human experts. By examining thousands of images, the system learns to distinguish between benign and malignant growths, providing doctors with invaluable insights that aid in diagnosis and treatment planning. This marriage of data and computation revolutionizes patient care, offering a glimpse into a future where technology and medicine work hand in hand to save lives.

Machine learning and deep learning continue to transform our world, each contributing its strengths to the technological landscape. Whether it's the simplicity and efficiency of machine learning in everyday applications or the profound capabilities of deep learning in tackling complex challenges, both play indispensable roles in the advancement of AI.

Neural Networks: The Brain Behind AI

Think of neural networks as the lifelines of deep learning, akin to the intricate web of neurons in our brains. This analogy isn't just poetic; it's quite literal. Neural networks are designed to mimic the way our brains process information. Imagine your brain considering whether to have a cup of coffee in the morning. It processes the desire for caffeine, the weather, your schedule, and even your energy levels from the day before. Similarly, neural networks process data through layers, each layer refining the information just a bit more until the final decision— or output—is made. These layers are known as the *input*, *hidden*, and *output* layers. Each serves a distinct function, working together to transform raw data into meaningful output.

At the core of a neural network lies its architecture, which is structured much like a layered cake, but one with a purpose beyond just satisfying your taste buds. The *input* layer receives raw data—imagine it as the first bite of that morning toast, crisp and untouched. This data is then passed through one or more *hidden* layers, where the real magic happens. Each *hidden* layer is a network of nodes, or artificial neurons, all equipped with an activation function that decides whether the information should be passed along. It's this process that allows the network to recognize complex patterns, much like how you might discern the nuanced flavors of a dish. Finally, the *output* layer presents the data's final interpretation, akin to taking the action to add a dash of salt or pepper to that dish.

To make sense of all this complexity, a visual representation can be incredibly helpful. Imagine a flowchart that starts with an initial input—say, a handwritten number. As the data flows through each layer, it becomes increasingly refined, emerging as a digit recognized with uncanny accuracy. Such diagrams are not just academic exercises; they are crucial tools for understanding how data transforms from raw input to a polished result. They illustrate how each node and layer contributes to the network's overarching goal of identifying patterns and making decisions.

However, it's crucial to acknowledge that while neural networks are powerful, they come with their own set of challenges and limitations. One of the most pressing issues is their insatiable appetite for data. Training a neural network requires a vast amount of information, a bit like teaching a person to read in a nonnative language by exposing them to thousands upon thousands of books. The more data you have, the better the network performs, but gathering such data can be both time-consuming and costly. Furthermore, these networks demand significant computational power, often requiring specialized hardware capable of handling massive calculations at high speeds.

Another limitation is the so-called "black-box" nature of deep learning models. While neural networks can be exceptionally effective at tasks like image and speech recognition, understanding why they make certain decisions is a bit like trying to decipher the inner workings of a magician's trick. You see the outcome, but the process remains shrouded in mystery. This opacity poses challenges, especially in fields like healthcare, where understanding the reasoning behind a diagnosis is as important as the diagnosis itself. Researchers are actively working to make these models more transparent, striving to shed light on the decision-making processes hidden within.

The world of neural networks is fascinatingly complex, blending elements of biology, mathematics, and computer science into a powerful tool capable of remarkable feats. Yet, as we continue to unlock its potential, it's crucial to remain mindful of the challenges that lie ahead, ensuring that this technology serves us in ways that are both innovative and responsible.

Big Data in AI

"Big Data" is a term that gets thrown around a lot, but what does it really mean? At its core, big data refers to massive volumes of information produced at high speed in a wide variety of formats. Imagine all the photos uploaded everywhere in the world on social media, along with the streams of data from smart devices, and the countless transactions completed online every second of the day. This colossal amount of information doesn't just sit idly by. It feeds into AI systems, acting as the lifeblood that allows these systems to learn, adapt, and improve. The sheer volume and speed at which data is generated today is mind-boggling. Without Big Data, AI would be like a racecar without fuel—packed with potential but unable to go anywhere.

The relationship between AI and Big Data is mutually beneficial. AI models thrive on data. The more data they consume, the smarter they become. This symbiotic relationship is what drives AI's rapid advancement. By processing vast datasets, AI systems can identify patterns and make predictions that were previously unimaginable. For example, in the world of finance, algorithms sift through oceans of market data to detect trends and make investment recommendations. In healthcare, AI analyzes patient records to forecast disease outbreaks or tailor personalized treatment plans. But this powerful capability hinges on the availability of large, diverse datasets. Without them, AI's ability to evolve and refine its understanding of complex problems would be severely limited.

So, where does all this data come from? The sources are as diverse as they are vast. User-generated content is a significant contributor. Every time you post on social media or comment on a blog, you're adding to the pool of Big Data. Then there's sensor data, which comes from an array of devices, from fitness trackers monitoring your steps to satellites capturing images of weather patterns. Transactional data, generated every time you make a purchase or complete an online form, also plays a vital role. Each data type offers unique insights, and when combined, they provide a rich tapestry of information that AI systems can analyze and learn from.

Managing Big Data, however, comes with challenges. One of the most pressing is data privacy and security. With so much personal information floating around, ensuring that it's protected from breaches or misuse is paramount. European Union laws like GDPR (General Data Protection Regulation) have been put in place to safeguard data privacy, but they can also pose barriers to data accessibility, slowing down AI development. Another hurdle is ensuring data quality and relevance. Not all data is useful. Some can be outdated or incorrect, leading to faulty AI outputs. Maintaining high data standards is crucial for AI systems to function effectively and deliver accurate results.

Big Data is an indispensable resource for AI, but it requires careful handling. As we continue to push the boundaries of what AI can achieve, the role of Big Data will only become more critical. The future of AI development hinges on our ability to manage this precious resource wisely, ensuring that it continues to fuel innovation while safeguarding the interests of individuals and society.

2

THE EVOLUTION OF AI

Let's go back in time about one hundred years, where we find ourselves in the company of a young British mathematician named Alan Turing as he scribbles away at his dusty desk, surrounded by stacks of papers adorned in cryptic symbols and complex equations. Little did the world know, but Turing was laying the groundwork for what would become one of the most transformative technologies of our time. His pioneering work in the 1930s and 1940s introduced concepts that still underpin AI today. Turing's vision of computing machinery capable of simulating human intelligence was revolutionary. He proposed the universal Turing machine, a theoretical construct that could simulate any computer algorithm, effectively laying the foundation for modern computing. But Turing didn't stop there. In 1950, he introduced the "Turing Test," a simple yet profound idea to evaluate a machine's ability to exhibit human-like intelligence. The test asks whether a machine can engage in a conversation that is indistinguishable from human interaction. While no AI has fully passed this test quite yet, it is around the corner, and it remains a benchmark for assessing machine intelligence that continues to inspire AI research and development.

Fast-forward to the summer of 1956, a time when Artificial Intelligence was officially christened as a field of study. Picture a group of bright minds gathered at Dartmouth College, led by mathematician John McCarthy. This meeting, known as the Dartmouth Conference, marked the birth of "artificial intelligence" as a formal discipline. The conference's goal was ambitious: to explore the idea that every aspect of learning and intelligence could be precisely described and simulated by a machine. This gathering sparked a surge of interest and investment in AI, leading to the creation of early AI programs that aimed to replicate human reasoning. One such program, the "Logic Theorist," developed by Allen Newell and Herbert Simon, was capable of proving mathematical theorems, demonstrating that machines could indeed perform tasks that required intellectual processes akin to human thinking. These early developments laid the groundwork for the decades of innovation that would follow, as researchers sought to push the boundaries of what machines could achieve.

As the 1970s and 1980s rolled around, AI began to mature, evolving from its embryonic stages into a more sophisticated field with diverse applications. This era witnessed the rise of symbolic AI and expert systems, which sought to replicate human expertise in specific domains—such as a system that could diagnose diseases or provide legal advice based on a set of rules and facts. These expert systems were among the first practical applications of AI, proving that machines could indeed mimic human decision-making in specialized areas. The development of AI programming languages like LISP and PROLOG further propelled the field, providing researchers with the tools needed to build increasingly complex systems. It was a time of great optimism, as AI enthusiasts envisioned a future where machines would seamlessly integrate into every aspect of our lives, augmenting our capabilities and enhancing our world.

The journey of AI was not without its hurdles, however. The field experienced setbacks as researchers grappled with the limitations of the technology and the complexity of human intelligence. Despite these setbacks, the 1990s saw a pivotal shift towards data-driven approaches, marking the dawn of modern AI. The convergence of increased computing power and the availability of vast datasets revolutionized the field, giving rise to "Machine Learning"—a method that allows computers to learn from data and improve their performance over time. This shift was driven by the realization that instead of hard-coding every rule and exception, machines could be trained to recognize patterns and make decisions based on data inputs. Machine learning became the cornerstone of AI research, enabling systems to tackle problems with unprecedented accuracy and efficiency. It's the reason why your smartphone can recognize your face, why your email can sort spam effectively, and why your streaming service can suggest movies you might enjoy. The rise of machine learning marked a new chapter in AI, one that continues to unfold as we harness the power of data to unlock the full potential of intelligent machines.

Key Breakthroughs That Shaped the Field

One of the most iconic moments in AI history occurred in 1997, when IBM's "Deep Blue" computer took on world chess champion Garry

Kasparov in a match that would forever alter our perception of machine intelligence. Deep Blue's victory was a turning point,

showcasing AI's ability to tackle complex, strategic tasks that were once the exclusive domain of human intellect. Using brute-force computing power and advanced algorithms, Deep Blue analyzed millions of potential moves, demonstrating that machines could compete and excel in games requiring immense foresight. This victory wasn't just about chess; it symbolized AI's growing capacity to challenge human expertise in various fields, raising questions about the limits of machine intelligence and the future of human-machine collaboration.

Fast-forward to 2011, and we see another AI marvel in action. IBM's "Watson" stepped onto the stage, not to play chess, but to compete in *Jeopardy!* — a game that requires more than just knowledge; it requires the ability to understand and respond to nuances in language. Watson's triumph over seasoned champions Ken Jennings and Brad Rutter was a testament to the advances in natural language processing and information retrieval. Unlike Deep Blue, which relied on sheer computational power, Watson demonstrated a nuanced understanding of language, parsing complex questions and retrieving relevant information from vast databases with remarkable speed and accuracy. This achievement underscored AI's potential to revolutionize industries like customer service, healthcare, and education, where understanding and interacting with humans is key.

Underlying these milestones are transformative technologies that have redefined the AI landscape. Convolutional neural networks (CNNs), for example, have revolutionized image processing, enabling machines to recognize objects, faces, and even emotions with human-like precision. These networks, inspired by the human visual cortex, have become the backbone of many AI applications, from autonomous vehicles to facial recognition systems. Their ability to process visual data has opened new frontiers in fields like security, entertainment, and medicine, where accurate image analysis is crucial. Meanwhile, advancements in natural language processing (NLP) have given rise to models like GPT, which power conversational collaborators and intelligent assistants. These models can generate coherent and contextually relevant text, making them invaluable tools for content creation, translation, and customer interaction.

AI's influence extends beyond entertainment and language; it's reshaping research and industry, particularly in genomics and drug discovery. AI algorithms can analyze genetic data at a scale and speed previously unimaginable, identifying patterns and anomalies that might lead to breakthroughs in understanding diseases. In drug discovery, AI accelerates the process by predicting how different compounds will interact with biological targets, potentially reducing the time and cost of bringing new drugs to market. These applications highlight AI's role as a catalyst for scientific innovation, driving progress in fields that directly impact human health and well-being.

AI is also making waves in manufacturing, where algorithmic automation is transforming production processes. Intelligent robots and machines now perform tasks with precision and efficiency, often surpassing human capabilities. This shift increases productivity and frees human workers from repetitive, mundane tasks, allowing them to focus on more creative and strategic roles. In this way, AI is not just replacing human labor but augmenting it, creating opportunities for humans and machines to work together in harmony. These advancements illustrate AI's potential to drive economic growth and improve quality of life, as it streamlines operations and enhances our ability to innovate in diverse sectors.

AI Across Industries

Artificial Intelligence has quietly woven itself into the fabric of various industries, each adoption as unique as the field itself. Take agriculture, for instance. Gone are the days when farming relied solely on intuition and manual labor. Today, AI is the backbone of precision farming, which optimizes the use of resources like water, fertilizers, and pesticides. Sensors and drones equipped with AI can monitor crop health in real-time, analyzing soil conditions and weather patterns to maximize yield while minimizing waste. This isn't just about growing more food—it's about doing it sustainably and intelligently. By reducing the guesswork, AI helps farmers make data-driven decisions that improve both the environment and their bottom line.

In the world of manufacturing, AI has found a home in predictive maintenance, a game-changer for factories around the globe. Imagine a production line where machines self-diagnose issues before they become costly breakdowns. AI sensors continuously monitor equipment health, predicting failures and scheduling maintenance only when necessary. This approach saves money and reduces downtime, ensuring that production flows smoothly. It's a far cry from the old "fix it when it breaks" mentality, offering a proactive solution that keeps the wheels of industry turning efficiently. By integrating AI into their operations, manufacturers can optimize their processes, extending the life of their machinery and enhancing productivity.

The financial sector has also embraced AI, particularly in the realm of fraud detection. Here, AI algorithms sift through mountains of transactions, identifying patterns and anomalies that might indicate fraudulent activity. This capability allows banks and financial institutions to spot fraud in real-time, protecting their clients and maintaining trust. But AI's influence doesn't stop there. It also powers customer service chatbots, personalizing user experiences and providing instant support. In a world where time is money, AI ensures that financial services are faster, smarter, and more secure than ever.

Healthcare has undergone a revolution thanks to AI, with diagnostics being one of the most significant transformations. AI algorithms analyze medical images, such as X-rays and MRIs, with remarkable accuracy, often matching or even surpassing human radiologists. This technology can detect diseases at earlier stages, enabling timely

21

treatment and better outcomes. AI systems flag potential health issues before they become serious, offering doctors a second pair of eyes in the diagnostic process. Beyond imaging, AI assists in crafting personalized treatment plans, considering a patient's genetic makeup and medical history. By tailoring healthcare to individual needs, AI is not just improving lives—it's saving them.

AI's reach extends into other niches, such as entertainment, where it plays a crucial role in content personalization. Streaming services like Netflix and Spotify use AI to analyze your viewing and listening habits, curating recommendations that suit your tastes. It's like having a personal curator who knows exactly what you want to watch or listen to next. This isn't just about convenience; it's about creating engaging experiences that keep users coming back for more. By learning from user interactions, AI keeps the entertainment industry dynamic and responsive, adapting to ever-changing consumer preferences.

Economically, AI's impact is immense, boosting growth and productivity across sectors. In logistics, for example, AI optimizes routes for delivery trucks, reducing fuel consumption and cutting costs. This efficiency translates to faster deliveries and happier customers. By automating routine tasks and streamlining operations, AI frees up human resources for more strategic roles, fostering innovation and growth. The ripple effect is felt throughout the economy, as businesses become more competitive and industries more resilient. AI isn't just a tool; it's a catalyst for progress, driving transformation at an unprecedented pace.

AI Winters and Their Impact

The history of AI isn't all triumphs and breakthroughs. Periods known as "AI winters" have punctuated the field's development, times when enthusiasm for Artificial Intelligence waned significantly. These were marked by sharp declines in funding and interest, casting a long shadow over AI research.

What caused these so-called "AI winters?" At their core, they stemmed from unrealistic expectations and overpromises. Enthusiastic predictions about what AI could achieve often missed the mark, leading to disappointment when reality didn't keep pace with imagination. In the early years, AI was hailed as a technology that would soon rival human intelligence in every aspect. Yet, despite initial progress, AI systems struggled with tasks requiring common sense and adaptability. The technology of the time simply couldn't support such lofty ambitions. Limitations in computing power, data availability, and algorithmic sophistication meant that many projects fell short of their goals. As the gap between expectation and reality widened, so did disillusionment among funders and the public, resulting in cutbacks and a significant reduction in support for AI research.

The most significant AI winters occurred between 1974–1980 and 1987–2000; and their consequences were profound, affecting not just the immediate research landscape but also the careers and livelihoods of many in the field. Funding cuts meant that many promising projects were shelved or abandoned altogether. Job opportunities in AI dried up, forcing talented researchers to pivot to other fields or leave academia entirely. In some ways, the AI community turned inward, focusing on more modest, achievable goals rather than the grand visions that had initially fueled the field's early growth. This introspection was not without its benefits. It led to a more cautious and realistic approach to AI research, laying the groundwork for future resilience and innovation.

The AI community recognized the need to balance ambition with practicality, ensuring that public and investor expectations aligned more closely with technological capabilities. This shift in mindset encouraged a more incremental approach to advancement, where success was measured not by sweeping revolutionary changes but by steady, meaningful progress. By focusing on achievable milestones and building on each success, researchers could maintain momentum even when faced with setbacks. This pragmatic approach has helped prevent a repeat of the cycles of hype and disappointment that characterized earlier eras.

Today, as AI enjoys a new spring, driven by machine learning and data science, the lessons of the past remain relevant. Researchers know that while AI holds enormous potential, it is imperative to communicate both its possibilities and limitations honestly. By doing so, they help foster a climate of trust and stability, ensuring that the field can weather future challenges without succumbing to the boom-and-bust cycles of the past. This perspective not only benefits the AI community, but also the industries and individuals who rely on AI technologies to drive innovation and solve complex problems.

3

AI TODAY

When we walk into a hospital these days the computers that hum quietly in the background are not simply tools, but partners in patient care. They run sophisticated AI systems that work seamlessly alongside doctors, enhancing the accuracy and speed of medical diagnostics. AI has emerged as a transformative force in healthcare, reshaping how diseases are detected and treated. This is happening now, and it's changing lives.

AI's role in diagnostics is nothing short of revolutionary. Consider the early detection of diseases like cancer, where time is of the essence. AI algorithms analyze medical images with uncanny precision, spotting anomalies that might escape the human eye. In radiology, deep learning models sift through countless X-rays, CT scans, and MRIs, identifying patterns and potential issues at a speed and accuracy previously unattainable. This rapid analysis enables earlier interventions, increasing the chances of successful treatment and reducing the burden on overworked medical staff. AI doesn't just stop at identifying problems; it aids in crafting solutions, ensuring that each diagnosis is backed by data-driven insights.

Personalized medicine is another area where AI shines, tailoring treatment plans to fit each patient's unique genetic makeup and medical history. Genomic data analysis, powered by AI, allows for personalized drug prescriptions, optimizing dosages to maximize effectiveness and minimize side effects. It's like having a custom-made suit, but for your health. Predictive analytics take this a step further, using patient-specific data to *anticipate* responses to treatments—a system that can suggest the best course of action based on your genetic profile and past medical experiences. This level of personalization promises to enhance patient outcomes, moving healthcare from a one-size-fits-all approach to something far more precise.

The impact of AI extends beyond treatment into the realm of medical research and development, accelerating the pace at which new drugs and therapies are discovered. AI-driven molecular analysis plays a crucial role in drug discovery, identifying potential compounds and predicting their interactions with biological targets. This reduces the time and cost involved in bringing new treatments to market. Similarly, AI optimizes clinical trials, selecting suitable candidates and predicting outcomes with greater accuracy. The control group in double-blind studies for new drugs can be digitally modeled by AI, eliminating the need to recruit people who are simply receiving a placebo rather than the potentially beneficial treatment. By reducing the guesswork, AI speeds up research and increases its success rate, saving lives by delivering effective treatments more quickly.

AI plays a pivotal role in patient management too. Wearable health devices, powered by AI, monitor vital signs in real-time, offering insights into a patient's health between doctor visits. These devices can alert healthcare providers to potential issues before they escalate, allowing for proactive care. Meanwhile, AI-powered virtual health assistants offer patients personalized advice and reminders, helping them manage chronic conditions and adhere to prescribed treatments.

AI in Finance

In the world of finance, risk assessment is the backbone of stability and confidence. AI has become a game-changer in this space, offering unprecedented accuracy and efficiency. Machine learning models analyze credit scores with pinpoint precision, sifting through vast amounts of financial data, learning from patterns and predicting creditworthiness more accurately than traditional methods. This doesn't just streamline the process; it minimizes errors, providing lenders with reliable insights into potential risks. Fraud detection, another critical aspect of risk management, benefits immensely from AI. Algorithms now monitor transactions in real-time, identifying suspicious activities before they wreak havoc. By distinguishing between legitimate and fraudulent transactions, AI helps protect both consumers and financial institutions from financial loss and reputational damage.

Trading, a realm often associated with fast-paced decisions and high stakes, has likewise been transformed by AI. Sophisticated trading algorithms harness the power of AI prediction models, allowing them to analyze market trends with incredible speed. These algorithms make split-second decisions that human traders simply can't match. The result? More efficient trading strategies that capitalize on market fluctuations. Real-time market analysis further enhances trading by providing up-to-the-minute insights. AI systems digest news, social media sentiment, and economic indicators, giving traders a comprehensive picture of the market landscape. This allows for more informed decisions, leading to better returns and reduced risks.

Customer service at financial institutions has undergone a revolution, too, thanks to AI. When a customer has a question about their bank account, instead of waiting in line or on hold, they can interact with a friendly chatbot. These AI-driven chatbots handle routine inquiries swiftly, providing instant assistance and freeing up human agents for more complex tasks. Beyond customer support, AI offers personalized advice, tailoring suggestions based on an individual's economic habits and goals. It's having a dedicated financial advisor available day and night, steering you to better money decisions without the hefty fees.

Compliance with financial regulations is non-negotiable, and AI plays a crucial role in ensuring that institutions adhere to these standards. Compliance monitoring systems powered by AI track regulatory changes and assess whether a bank's operations align with legal requirements. These systems can process vast amounts of regulations, identifying areas that need attention and alerting compliance officers before issues arise. AI tools designed for anti-money laundering practices further enhance compliance by analyzing transaction patterns and flagging potential illicit activities. This proactive approach not only prevents regulatory breaches but also protects institutions from hefty fines and reputational damage.

Case Study - Credit Risk Assessment

Let's examine how AI improves credit risk assessment. Traditional methods rely heavily on historical data and fixed criteria, often missing nuances that could indicate a borrower's true potential. AI, however, goes beyond the surface. By analyzing a broader set of data points, including spending habits, social media activity, and even mobile phone usage, AI models paint a more accurate picture of creditworthiness. This comprehensive approach reduces default rates and opens lending opportunities to those who might be overlooked by conventional assessments. In practice, a leading bank implemented AI-driven credit scoring and saw a 20% reduction in default rates within the first year. This success highlights AI's transformative power in risk management, making financial services more inclusive and reliable.

AI in Retail

Imagine walking into a store where every product seems to have been picked just for you. This may soon be your new shopping experience, driven by the magic of robotics and AI personalization. Retailers already use sophisticated recommendation engines to tailor shopping experiences to individual preferences. These engines analyze your past purchases, browsing history, and even your social media interactions to suggest products you're apt to appreciate—like having a personal shopper who knows your style and taste. This kind of personalization enhances customer satisfaction and boosts sales, as shoppers are more inclined to purchase items that resonate with their values. Dynamic pricing strategies further refine this experience. By leveraging AI analytics, retailers adjust prices in real time, considering factors like demand, competitor pricing, and customer behavior. This flexibility ensures competitive pricing while maximizing profits, creating a win-win for both retailers and consumers.

In the bustling world of retail, inventory management can make or break a business. This is where AI steps in, optimizing stock levels and streamlining supply chain operations with precision. Predictive analytics play a pivotal role in demand forecasting, allowing retailers to anticipate customer needs before they arise. By analyzing historical sales data, patterns, and market trends, AI models predict which products will be in demand and when, ensuring that shelves are always stocked with the right items at the right time. Automated replenishment systems take this a step further, ordering stock automatically when levels dip below a certain threshold. This automation reduces human error and minimizes the risk of overstocking or understocking, saving time and resources while enhancing operational efficiency.

Customer service is another realm where AI leaves its mark, transforming interactions into seamless, satisfying experiences. You can have a virtual shopping assistant that guides you through your online shopping journey, offering real-time advice and product recommendations based on your preferences. These AI-driven assistants provide personalized support, answering questions and assisting with purchases. Meanwhile, AI-driven sentiment analysis interprets customer feedback, sifting through reviews and social media comments to glean insights into customer satisfaction. This analysis helps retailers understand consumer sentiments, allowing them to adapt their offerings and address concerns promptly. By leveraging AI, retailers ensure that each interaction leaves customers feeling valued and understood.

Marketing strategies have also evolved as AI enhances campaigns that boost customer engagement. AI algorithms power targeted advertising, delivering personalized ads to consumers based on their behavior. This targeted approach increases the likelihood of conversion, as customers are more likely to engage with content that speaks directly to them. Customer segmentation and profiling take this personalization further, categorizing shoppers into distinct groups based on their demographics, purchasing habits, and preferences. By understanding these segments, retailers can craft marketing messages that resonate with each group, fostering loyalty and driving sales. AI's ability to process data quickly and accurately enables marketers to fine-tune their strategies, ensuring that every campaign hits its mark.

The integration of AI in retail isn't just about technology; it's about enhancing the human element of shopping. By tailoring experiences, optimizing operations, and personalizing interactions, AI brings a level of sophistication and efficiency that elevates the entire retail landscape.

AI in Transportation

We are moments away from a world where cars drive themselves, and traffic jams are a relic of the past; where delivery-bots cruise along sidewalks with take-out orders and offices supplies. This isn't a scene from *The Jetsons*; it's already becoming our reality thanks to AI-driven autonomous vehicles. These self-driving marvels are equipped with advanced systems that allow them to navigate complex environments with precision. At the heart of this technology are sophisticated AI algorithms dedicated to navigation and obstacle detection. These algorithms act as the vehicle's brain, processing data from sensors and cameras in real-time to make split-second decisions. Whether recognizing pedestrians or adjusting to sudden changes in traffic flow, these systems enhance safety by minimizing human error. Reliability remains paramount, so autonomous vehicles undergo rigorous testing to ensure they perform consistently under various conditions. Each test fine-tunes their ability to interpret the world around them, making them safer and more efficient with every iteration.

Beyond the individual car, AI is transforming entire cities through smarter traffic management. With urban areas growing denser, efficient traffic flow becomes crucial. AI steps in with smart traffic lights that use real-time data to optimize signal timings. These signals adjust themselves based on current traffic conditions, smoothing out congestion and reducing wait times—creating a city where green lights seem to magically align with your route. In addition, real-time traffic monitoring systems provide city planners with invaluable data, enabling them to predict and alleviate bottlenecks before they occur. By analyzing patterns and anticipating surges, AI helps keep our roads less congested and our commutes more predictable.

Logistics and delivery services are also reaping the benefits of AI integration. Delivery trucks can now chart the most efficient routes, cutting down on fuel costs and delivery times. AI-driven route optimization considers factors like traffic, weather, and even road conditions to ensure packages reach their destinations swiftly. This precision boosts efficiency and reduces the environmental impact. Within warehouses, AI manages inventory with similar precision. Automated systems track stock levels and organize items for quick retrieval, minimizing human error and enhancing productivity. By streamlining these processes, AI ensures that supply chains remain robust and responsive to demand fluctuations.

Looking to the skies, AI is set to revolutionize delivery systems through the use of drones. These airborne couriers promise to bypass traditional traffic woes entirely, delivering packages directly to your doorstep. Equipped with AI navigation systems, drones can plot courses that avoid obstacles and ensure safe deliveries, even in crowded urban environments.

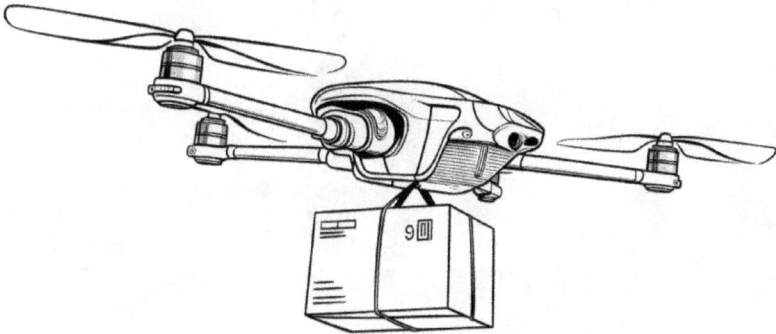

Meanwhile, on the ground, the "hyperloop" concept, introduced by Elon Musk in 2012 as a "fifth mode of transportation," would use AI to offer unprecedented speed and safety. Hyperloops involve capsules riding on air bearings inside depressurized tubes driven by linear induction motors—promising to move people and goods at lightning speeds, with AI ensuring optimal operation and safety.

The impact of AI on transportation, medicine, financial services, and retail is profound, offering solutions that extend beyond convenience to include safety, efficiency, and environmental sustainability, which invites us to consider the limitless possibilities that lie ahead. Yet, there are ethical and moral questions that cannot be ignored.

4

ETHICS

P icture this: you're walking through a bustling city center, surrounded by the familiar sounds of urban life. But look up and you might notice the ever-watchful eye of AI-powered surveillance systems. These systems are designed to keep us safe, yet they also raise a serious question: *who's watching the watchers?*

AI's ability to collect and analyze personal data is both its greatest strength and its most significant ethical challenge. From facial recognition cameras in public spaces to social media platforms that mine your data for targeted ads, AI technologies are weaving themselves into the fabric of our daily lives, often without our explicit consent or understanding.

These systems, by design, harvest vast amounts of data to discern patterns, forecast behaviors, or sometimes bolster security. However, this strength also poses a risk. The same algorithms that tailor movie suggestions can craft intricate personal profiles, potentially overstepping privacy boundaries. The crux of the problem lies in the algorithms' reliance on extensive datasets for effective training, escalating the likelihood of data breaches or misuse, thus exposing individuals to heightened surveillance and profiling risks.

To address these concerns, regulatory frameworks have been established, aiming to strike a balance between innovation and privacy protection. The European Union's General Data Protection Regulation (GDPR) is one such initiative. It mandates transparency about data processing and allows individuals to opt-out of significant automated decisions, giving people more control over their information. Similarly, the California Consumer Privacy Act (CCPA) extends these rights to residents of California, requiring businesses to disclose what personal data they collect and how it's used. These regulations reflect a growing recognition of the need to safeguard privacy in an era where data is a commodity. Yet, even with these laws in place, questions about enforcement and global applicability remain.

Consent and data ownership are pivotal issues in the AI ethics debate. When you click "agree" to a platform's terms and conditions, do you truly understand what you're allowing? Many digital platforms employ complex user consent mechanisms that can obscure the full extent of data usage. This often leaves users in the dark about how their information is being leveraged. The debate over data ownership rights further complicates matters. If your personal data powers an AI system, do you have a stake in the outcomes it produces? This question is at the heart of discussions around ethical AI, pushing us to reconsider concepts of ownership in the digital age.

Protecting privacy in AI systems requires proactive strategies. Anonymization techniques, which strip data of identifiable information, offer one approach. By ensuring that data cannot be traced back to individuals, these methods can mitigate privacy risks while maintaining the utility of datasets for AI training. However, even anonymized data can sometimes be re-identified to individuals, so continuous vigilance is needed. Privacy-preserving machine learning models represent another frontier. These models are designed to perform complex analyses without exposing sensitive data, offering a promising path forward as we seek to balance privacy with technological advancement.

Reflection on Privacy in Your Life

Take a moment to reflect on your digital footprint. Consider the apps and platforms you use daily—how much personal information have you willingly shared? Jot down your thoughts on how this data might be used. This exercise can help you become more aware of privacy concerns, empowering you to make informed decisions in your digital interactions.

AI and Bias

Imagine you're applying for a job, and the decision rests in the hands of an AI system. It sounds efficient, but what if the algorithm is biased? AI systems, despite their cutting-edge technology, can inherit biases from the data they are trained on. These biases can lead to discriminatory outcomes, affecting decisions in hiring, lending, and even criminal sentencing. It often starts with biased training data—data that reflect existing societal prejudices. For example, if an AI is trained on resumes predominantly from one gender or ethnicity, it might favor those demographics when making decisions. Bias doesn't just stop at unfair hiring practices; it can ripple across society, reinforcing stereotypes and widening existing divides. The implications are profound, as biased algorithms can perpetuate and even exacerbate inequality, making it crucial to understand and address these issues.

Let's explore some real-world examples where AI bias has caused significant problems. Facial recognition technology is increasingly used in security and law enforcement. But studies have shown that these systems often exhibit racial bias, misidentifying people of color at higher rates than white individuals. This can lead to wrongful accusations and arrests, highlighting a severe flaw in systems meant to ensure public safety. Another example lies in algorithmic hiring practices. Some companies have used AI to screen job applicants, only to find that their systems favored male candidates over female ones. This occurred because the algorithms were trained on historical data where men dominated certain fields, leading to a cycle that continues to marginalize women in the workplace. These instances underscore the urgent need for vigilance and reform in AI applications.

Addressing bias in AI requires deliberate and proactive strategies. One crucial step is ensuring that the data used to train AI models is diverse and representative of all groups. By collecting data that accurately reflects the variety and complexity of human society, we can help mitigate bias from the start. Another approach involves implementing algorithmic fairness interventions. These are techniques designed to audit and adjust models, ensuring they perform equitably across different demographics. Regular audits can identify bias and allow developers to tweak models accordingly. Transparency in AI model development is also essential. By making the inner workings of AI systems accessible and understandable, stakeholders can identify potential biases and work to correct them. Such transparency builds trust and accountability, fostering a more inclusive and fair AI landscape.

The demographic composition of an AI development team plays a significant role in minimizing bias. Diverse teams bring a wealth of perspectives that can challenge assumptions and prevent blind spots in AI design. Inclusive design practices encourage the consideration of different user needs and experiences, reducing the risk of unintentional bias. Cross-disciplinary collaboration further enhances this process by integrating insights from fields like sociology, psychology, and ethics into AI development. By drawing on expertise from various domains, AI systems can be designed with a more holistic understanding of human behavior and societal dynamics. This collaborative approach ensures that AI serves everyone, not just a privileged few.

Creating AI systems that are free from bias is a complex challenge, but it is one that we must tackle head-on. By understanding the sources of bias and implementing strategies to counteract them, we can work towards AI that is truly fair and equitable. This involves not only technical solutions but also a commitment to diversity and inclusion at every step of the AI development process. As AI becomes more embedded in our lives, the importance of addressing bias cannot be overstated. It calls for diligence, creativity, and a willingness to confront uncomfortable truths.

Ethical AI

If you were using an AI program that's making critical decisions about your healthcare or finances, wouldn't you want to know how it works and whether it's treating you fairly? That's where ethical AI principles step in, guiding the development and use of these systems to ensure they operate in ways that respect human values.

At the heart of ethical AI lies the commitment to fairness, accountability, and transparency. Fairness ensures that AI systems offer equal opportunities and do not discriminate against any group. Accountability involves holding developers and organizations responsible for the impacts of their AI applications. Transparency means making AI systems understandable and their workings clear, so that users can trust the decisions made by these machines.

Frameworks have been established to guide the ethical deployment of AI. Take, for example, the Institute of Electrical and Electronics Engineers' (IEEE) "Ethically Aligned Design," which provides a comprehensive set of guidelines to ensure AI respects human rights and promotes well-being. The IEEE framework emphasizes the importance of embedding ethical considerations into every stage of AI development, from design to deployment. Meanwhile, the European Union's Ethics Guidelines for Trustworthy AI offer another layer of guidance, proposing that AI should be lawful, ethical, and robust. These guidelines stress that AI systems must be developed with a focus on transparency, accountability, and continuous oversight, ensuring they serve people rather than control them. Such frameworks are crucial as they provide a reference point for developers and policymakers, helping to align AI innovations with societal values.

Transparency in AI is not just a "nice-to-have;" it's a necessity. If an AI system makes a mistake, how can we correct it if we don't understand why it reached its decision? Explainable AI techniques aim to tackle this challenge by making AI systems more interpretable. They provide insights into how AI models arrive at their decisions, offering users and developers the ability to understand the reasoning behind the outputs. This transparency builds trust, allowing people to rely on AI without fear of hidden biases or errors. Additionally, open-source AI initiatives play a significant role in promoting transparency. By making AI tools and models publicly accessible, these initiatives invite scrutiny and collaboration, fostering innovation while ensuring that AI systems remain accountable to the communities they serve.

The question of accountability looms large in discussions about AI ethics. When an AI system fails, who should be held responsible? Establishing accountability mechanisms is crucial to address this question. Auditing AI systems for compliance is one way to ensure they align with ethical standards. Regular audits can uncover biases or errors, allowing developers to rectify issues before they cause harm. However, audits alone aren't enough. It's also vital to establish clear lines of responsibility within organizations. This means defining who is accountable for different aspects of AI development and operation, from data collection to model deployment. By assigning responsibility, organizations can ensure that ethical considerations are prioritized and that any problems are addressed promptly.

Navigating the maze of ethical AI requires a multifaceted approach, blending technical solutions with a commitment to human-centric design, creating systems that that respect and enhances human dignity. This involves aligning AI development with ethical principles, ensuring that as technology evolves, it remains a force for good. As we continue to innovate, keeping these ethics at the forefront will ensure that AI contributes positively to society, empowering individuals and communities while safeguarding their rights and interests.

AI and Employment - Threat or Opportunity?

In the ever-evolving landscape of employment, AI stands as both a disruptor and a creator. On one hand, AI technologies are reshaping the job market by automating routine tasks that were once the domain of human workers, like a factory floor where robots assemble products with precision, tirelessly working around the clock without breaks. Automation in sectors like manufacturing and transportation is becoming the norm, leading to increased efficiency but also sparking fears of job displacement. Administrative and clerical roles, too, find themselves in the crosshairs of automation. Tasks that involve data entry or simple decision-making are increasingly handled by AI, freeing up human resources for more complex and creative endeavors. However, this shift raises concerns about the future of work and the fate of those whose jobs are at risk.

Yet, within this disruption lies the seed of opportunity. AI is not just taking jobs; it's creating them, albeit in areas that require a different set of skills. The tech industry, in particular, is experiencing a boom in roles related to AI and machine learning. As AI systems become more prevalent, the demand for skilled workers to develop, maintain, and improve these systems is on the rise. New job roles are emerging, from AI researchers and data scientists to AI ethicists who ensure that technology aligns with societal values. These roles are not just confined to tech companies; industries across the board are seeking talent that can bridge the gap between traditional practices and AI-driven innovation. This transformation highlights the need for adaptability and a workforce that is prepared to embrace new challenges.

As AI continues to influence the job market, the importance of skill development cannot be overstated. Reskilling and upskilling have become buzzwords in the age of AI, emphasizing the need for individuals to continuously update their capabilities. Educational programs and courses tailored to AI-related skills are popping up, providing opportunities for workers to pivot into new careers. Online platforms offer courses in coding, data analysis, and AI principles, making it easier than ever to learn from the comfort of your home. Lifelong learning initiatives encourage individuals to remain curious and proactive, equipping them with the tools needed to thrive in a digital economy. By investing in education and training, workers can position themselves advantageously within an AI-driven world.

AI's influence on the job market isn't solely about replacing human labor; it also drives economic growth through the expansion of AI-related services and industries. As AI technologies advance, they open new avenues for business and innovation. The healthcare sector, for example, is seeing growth in AI applications that enhance diagnostics and patient care, creating demand for professionals who can implement and manage these systems. Finance, retail, and entertainment are similarly benefiting from AI's capabilities, leading to the development of specialized services that cater to evolving consumer needs. This expansion fosters a dynamic job market where creativity and innovation are prized, offering opportunities for those willing to explore uncharted territories.

In navigating the intersection of AI and employment, we must recognize both the challenges and opportunities presented by this technological shift. While AI may displace certain roles, it also paves the way for new careers and economic growth. The key lies in adaptability and the willingness to embrace change. As we move forward, the focus should be on empowering individuals with the skills and knowledge needed to succeed in an AI-enhanced world. This balance between disruption and creation will shape the future of work, guiding us toward a landscape where humans and machines collaborate to achieve unprecedented advancements.

5
TOOLS & TECHNIQUES

A t the edge of a vast digital landscape, where every possibility seems within reach, you will find "TensorFlow," a powerful and freely available tool that has become a cornerstone of AI development. Created by the innovative minds at Google Brain, TensorFlow is an open-source library that simplifies the complex world of machine learning. Picture it as a versatile toolbox, offering everything you need to build intelligent systems that can learn and adapt. Its architecture is based on a data flow graph, which allows it to perform computations efficiently across multiple platforms. This means you can develop AI models that work seamlessly on everything from desktop computers to smartphones and even the cloud. In essence, TensorFlow is your gateway to exploring deep learning in ways that were once unimaginable.

What makes TensorFlow truly stand out among developers is its flexibility—a fluid architecture supports a wide range of tasks, from image recognition to natural language processing. Whether you're interested in building a model that can identify objects in photos or one that understands human speech, TensorFlow has you covered. One of its unique features is its high-level APIs, which provide a user-friendly interface for rapid prototyping. This means you can focus on creating innovative solutions without getting bogged down by technical complexities. Additionally, TensorFlow's seamless integration with Keras, Google's open-source library for artificial neural networks, makes it easier to build and train models, further enhancing its appeal to developers of all skill levels. The library's extensive tensor operations and automatic differentiation capabilities allow for sophisticated gradient calculations, giving you the tools to optimize and refine your models with precision.

In the realm of healthcare, TensorFlow is being used to develop AI models that predict disease outcomes, transforming how doctors and researchers approach patient care—analyzing vast datasets of medical records, identifying patterns that can forecast the likelihood of diseases like diabetes or heart conditions. By providing early warnings, these models empower healthcare professionals to take preventive measures, improving patient outcomes and reducing healthcare costs. In the finance sector, TensorFlow is being used to analyze market trends and predict risks, enabling financial institutions to make informed decisions that safeguard investments. This predictive power helps companies navigate economic uncertainties, ensuring stability and growth. Retailers are also leveraging TensorFlow to create personalized recommendation systems.

For those eager to dive into TensorFlow (which is open-source), there are numerous resources available to help you get started. Online platforms like Coursera and Udacity offer comprehensive courses that guide you through the basics of TensorFlow, providing hands-on experience in building AI models. These courses are designed to accommodate learners of all levels, whether you're a beginner looking to understand the fundamentals or a seasoned developer aiming to refine your skills. The official TensorFlow documentation is another invaluable resource, offering detailed guides and tutorials that cover a wide range of topics. Community forums, such as the TensorFlow Subreddit, provide a platform for you to connect with other developers, share ideas, and troubleshoot issues. Engaging with the TensorFlow community can be immensely rewarding, as you'll have access to a wealth of knowledge and support from like-minded individuals who are passionate about AI.

In exploring TensorFlow, you're not just learning about a tool; you're unlocking the potential to create intelligent systems that can change the world. Whether you're interested in healthcare, finance, retail, or any other industry, TensorFlow can offer the resources and support you need to bring your AI aspirations to life.

Natural Language Processing

We are entering a world where machines can effortlessly understand and interpret human language, bridging the gap between technology and communication. This is the realm of Natural Language Processing, or NLP. At its core, NLP is about enabling computers to understand, interpret, and respond to human language in a way that is both meaningful and useful. It's the magic behind your virtual assistants like Amazon Alexa and Google Assistant, answering your queries and managing your schedules with seeming ease. But its significance goes beyond convenience; NLP is transforming how we interact with technology, making it more intuitive and responsive to our needs.

In your everyday life, NLP powers a range of tech solutions that have become almost indispensable. Virtual assistants are a prime example, using NLP to process your spoken words and convert them into data that the system can understand and act upon. This involves not just recognizing individual words but understanding context and intent. NLP is also the backbone of chatbots used in customer service. These chatbots handle inquiries, troubleshoot problems, and even provide recommendations, often without the need for human intervention. This streamlines customer support, making it faster and more efficient, which is a win-win for businesses and consumers.

NLP relies on several sophisticated techniques and models to achieve its goals. Sentiment analysis is one such technique, used to gauge the mood or opinion behind a piece of text. For instance, businesses use sentiment analysis to understand customer feedback, discerning whether it's positive, negative, or neutral. This insight helps companies refine their products and services to better meet customer expectations. Another key technique is known as "entity recognition," which extracts information from text based on recognized data points, such as names, dates, or locations. This is crucial for organizing and retrieving information efficiently. Meanwhile, language generation models like GPT (Generative Pre-trained Transformer) take NLP a step further by creating text that is coherent and contextually relevant. These models are used in applications ranging from content creation to virtual storytelling, showcasing NLP's versatility and potential.

Despite its advancements, NLP faces challenges that stem from the inherent complexities of human language. Context and ambiguity are two major hurdles. Humans instinctively understand context, such as sarcasm or cultural references, but teaching a machine to do the same is incredibly difficult. Words can have multiple meanings depending on the situation, and NLP systems must discern the intended meaning to respond accurately. This challenge is being addressed through the development of more sophisticated models, like transformer-based architectures—which use a mechanism called "self-attention" to understand the context and relationships between different parts of a given sequence—can have significantly improved language understanding. These models, such as BERT and GPT-3, excel at processing context, offering more nuanced and accurate interpretations of text.

The rise of transformer models marks a significant advancement in NLP, pushing the boundaries of what machines can achieve. They have transformed NLP by enhancing the precision and consistency of language processing, making it possible to extract relevant information from large datasets more efficiently. However, as we push forward, ongoing innovations continue to refine these systems, addressing challenges like bias in data and the need for more comprehensive context understanding. The future of NLP looks promising as we explore new frontiers, seeking to make interactions with machines as natural and seamless as conversations with friends.

Data Mining

Consider data mining as a modern-day treasure hunt, where the treasure isn't gold or jewels, but valuable insights buried within trillions of bits of data. In sifting through mountains of information, we uncover patterns that aren't immediately obvious. That's what data mining does. It's a critical process for revealing hidden relationships in large datasets, making it indispensable for AI development. With techniques like clustering, classification, and association, data mining allows us to group similar data points, categorize them, and find associations that can inform decision-making. In essence, it's about transforming raw data into meaningful, actionable insights.

To navigate this complex landscape, you'll find a range of tools designed to make data mining more accessible. RapidMiner, for instance, offers a user-friendly interface that simplifies the mining process, even for those without a deep technical background. It's like having a guide who can help you chart a course through dense data jungles. Apache Mahout, on the other hand, provides scalable algorithms, designed to handle enormous datasets. These tools employ decision trees, which visualize decisions and their possible consequences, and neural networks, which mimic the human brain's neural connections to identify patterns and trends. Each method has its strengths, and the choice of tool often depends on the specific problem you're trying to solve.

Data mining finds applications in a myriad of sectors, each with its unique challenges and opportunities. In retail, market basket analysis is a technique that helps businesses understand consumer behavior by examining the products that customers frequently purchase together. This insight allows retailers to optimize product placement and promotions, enhancing sales and customer satisfaction. Meanwhile, in the finance sector, anomaly detection is a powerful tool for fraud detection. By analyzing transactional data, it can identify irregular patterns that may indicate fraudulent activity, enabling banks to act swiftly and protect their clients. These examples highlight how data mining can drive efficiency and innovation across industries.

However, with great power comes great responsibility. The ethical implications of data mining practices are substantial and can't be overlooked. Data privacy and consent are paramount concerns. Informed consent should be the cornerstone of any data mining initiative, with users fully aware of how their data will be used. Additionally, bias in data collection and interpretation poses a significant risk. If the data being analyzed is not representative of the population or is skewed in some way, the insights drawn from it can perpetuate stereotypes and lead to unfair outcomes. This is especially concerning in sectors like finance and healthcare, where biased decisions can have serious repercussions.

Reflection on Ethical Data Mining Practices

Think about the data you interact with daily. How is it collected? What are the potential ethical concerns? What steps can you take to ensure ethical practices in your work or personal projects? Consider privacy settings, informed consent, and the diversity of datasets. Reflection on your personal experience may help you recognize the importance of ethical data handling and the impact it can have on individuals and society.

The Power of Algorithms

At the heart of artificial intelligence lies a concept that's both simple and profound: algorithms. Picture algorithms as a set of instructions, much like a recipe you follow to bake a cake. They're the unsung heroes in the world of AI, providing the rules and guidelines that machines use to solve problems and perform tasks. These mathematical formulas allow computers to process data, learn from it, and make decisions. Essentially, algorithms are the backbone of AI systems, driving the learning and decision-making processes that enable machines to mimic human thought. Whether it's predicting tomorrow's weather or playing a game of chess, it's all about the algorithms running behind the scenes.

Supervised learning algorithms are crucial in AI development. These include linear regression and decision trees, which are used to predict outcomes based on input data. Imagine you're trying to determine the price of a house. A linear regression model could analyze factors like location, size, and age to predict its value. Decision trees, on the other hand, work by splitting data into branches based on different criteria, simplifying complex decision-making processes. Unsupervised learning algorithms, like "k-means clustering," first developed by an engineer at Bell Labs in the late 1950s, don't rely on labeled data. Instead, they find patterns and group similar items together. For instance, *k-means clustering* could help a retailer segment their customers based on purchasing behavior. Reinforcement learning models are another fascinating category, where machines learn by trial and error, much like how you might train a pet with rewards. These models are ideal for dynamic decision-making tasks, such as teaching a robot to navigate a new environment.

Recent advancements in algorithmic design have pushed the boundaries of what AI can achieve. Deep reinforcement learning is one such innovation, allowing machines to tackle complex tasks that require a sequence of decisions. This approach combines the strengths of deep learning, which excels at handling large amounts of data, with reinforcement learning's focus on action-oriented tasks. This produces systems that can learn strategies for games or optimize robotic movements with remarkable efficiency. Meanwhile, evolutionary algorithms draw inspiration from natural selection, evolving solutions over time through processes of mutation and selection. This method is particularly effective in solving optimization problems, where the goal is to find the best possible solution from a vast number of possibilities.

Looking ahead, the future of algorithmic development promises even more exciting possibilities. Quantum computing is poised to revolutionize algorithm speed and efficiency. By leveraging the principles of quantum mechanics, quantum computers can process information at unprecedented speeds, solving problems that would take classical computers centuries to crack. These light speed algorithms can analyze vast datasets almost instantaneously, opening new avenues in fields like cryptography and drug discovery. Another trend is the integration of AI algorithms with the "Internet of Things" (IoT)—physical objects and systems connected to the web.

As devices become more interconnected, algorithms will play a crucial role in managing and interpreting the data they generate, enhancing everything from smart homes to industrial automation.

The power of algorithms lies not just in their ability to process information, but in their potential to transform industries and reshape our everyday lives. As we continue to develop and refine these mathematical marvels, we unlock new opportunities for innovation and growth. Algorithms are more than just lines of code; they are the driving force behind AI's evolution, guiding machines as they learn, adapt, and grow. With each advancement, we move closer to a future where intelligent systems enhance our world in ways we've only imagined.

6

AI IN EVERYDAY LIFE

I t's a typical morning. You're rushing around, trying to remember if you locked the back door, fed the dog, advanced the laundry, while also wondering about the weather. In the swirl of this daily chaos, you ask, "Alexa, what's my schedule?" Your faithful AI assistant responds, listing your appointments and even suggesting you grab an umbrella because rain is on the horizon. These AI assistants are already at work, transforming how we manage our daily lives.

AI assistants like Amazon Alexa, Apple Siri, and Google Assistant have become household staples, thanks to their ability to understand and respond to voice commands. They operate using a blend of voice recognition and natural language processing (NLP), enabling them to interpret spoken language and provide relevant responses. By integrating with smart home devices and other services, these assistants offer a centralized hub for managing everything from your lights to your calendar. The technology behind them involves complex subsystems, including speech recognition, which converts audio into text, and natural language understanding, which interprets the text to determine your intent. This intricate process makes it possible for a simple voice command to trigger a series of actions tailored to your needs.

Amazon Alexa, for instance, is renowned for its vast array of "Skills"—a library of over 100,000 apps mostly made by third-party developers that can help with meal ideas, fitness, fact-checking, and much more. These "Skills" extend Alexa's functionality beyond basic tasks. By integrating with third-party apps, Alexa can do everything from ordering a pizza to controlling your smart thermostat. It uses machine learning to recognize various accents and phrasing, ensuring that it understands you, no matter how you speak. Apple Siri, on the other hand, is deeply woven into the iOS ecosystem, offering seamless connectivity across Apple devices. Its ability to sync with your iPhone, iPad, and Mac means you can start a task on one device and finish it on another without missing a beat. Google Assistant stands out for its context-aware responses, which allow it to remember past interactions and provide more personalized answers. This feature makes it not just reactive but proactive, anticipating your needs based on previous requests.

The practical applications of AI assistants are vast. They excel at setting reminders and managing schedules, ensuring you never miss a meeting or forget an important task. Whether you're home or on the go, they offer quick answers to questions, providing information on anything from traffic conditions to trivia. Moreover, their ability to control smart home devices means you can adjust your environment with just your voice, turning off lights, adjusting temperature, or locking doors without lifting a finger. This convenience streamlines your day, giving you more time to focus on what truly matters.

The rise of AI assistants that are aware of our every move has raised alarm, particularly concerning our privacy and security. Are we being watched by Big Data algorithms? While companies like Amazon and Google encrypt user data and offer options to delete voice recordings, privacy advocates still urge caution. Security vulnerabilities in connected devices also present risks, as hackers could potentially exploit them to gain unauthorized access to your home network. These concerns underscore the importance of staying informed about the technology you use and taking steps to protect your data.

Reflection on Balancing Convenience and Privacy

Consider the balance between convenience and privacy in your use of AI assistants. Reflect on the extent to which you're comfortable sharing personal information with these devices. Are there settings you can adjust to enhance your privacy? Think about the trade-offs involved and how they align with your values. This reflection will help you make informed choices about your interactions with technology.

Smart Homes

At its core, a smart home is a network of connected devices that communicate with each other, working harmoniously to enhance your comfort and convenience. AI-driven automation is a key player here, optimizing energy use and personalizing your home environment based on your habits. By analyzing data from various sensors and devices, AI systems can learn your routines, adjusting settings to save energy and improve efficiency without sacrificing comfort.

Smart thermostats like the Nest Learning Thermostat exemplify the impact of AI in home automation. These devices don't just regulate temperature; they learn from your preferences and adjust automatically, ensuring optimal comfort while minimizing energy consumption. Intelligent lighting systems, such as Philips Hue, offer similar benefits. By integrating with AI, these lights can change color and brightness based on time of day, mood, or even the content you're watching. Imagine your living room lights dimming to create the perfect ambiance for a movie night, all orchestrated by AI. Then there are AI-powered security systems with facial recognition capabilities. These systems monitor your home, detecting unfamiliar faces and alerting you to potential intrusions, providing peace of mind whether you're home or away. Together, these devices illustrate how AI transforms our living spaces into responsive, intuitive environments.

The benefits of smart homes extend beyond convenience. AI improves energy management by creating automated routines for lighting and temperature control. These routines can reduce energy waste, saving you money on utility bills and contributing to a greener planet. Enhanced security is another advantage, with AI monitoring your home for unusual activity, sending real-time alerts to your phone if something's amiss. This level of vigilance can deter intruders and ensure that your home remains a safe haven. Additionally, smart homes offer unparalleled convenience. Picture waking up to a home that adjusts to your morning routine, with your coffee brewing as your blinds open to let in natural light. This seamless integration of technology and daily life is what makes smart homes so appealing.

However, as with any technological advancement, smart homes come with their own set of challenges. One significant issue is interoperability. With so many devices and platforms on the market, ensuring that everything works together can be a headache. You might find that your smart thermostat doesn't communicate with your lighting system, leading to a fragmented experience. This lack of standardization can frustrate users and limit the full potential of smart home technology. Another concern is privacy. Continuous data collection is inherent to smart home devices, as they rely on user data to function effectively. While this data can enhance personalization and efficiency, it also raises questions about how it's stored and who has access to it.

Social Media

You've seen how scrolling on your favorite social media app seems eerily tailored to your interests. From the cat videos to the latest news articles, everything seems handpicked just for you. That's the power of AI at play. Social media platforms like Facebook and Instagram use sophisticated algorithms to personalize your feed, making it more engaging and relevant. These algorithms analyze your interactions, likes, shares, and even the time you spend on each post to create a customized experience. By learning your preferences, they deliver content that keeps you hooked, sometimes for hours on end—which can lead to addiction. Targeted advertising takes this a step further, using AI-driven data analysis to serve ads that align with your interests, often predicting your needs before you even realize them.

However, this personalization comes with a downside, often leading to the formation of echo chambers—information bubbles where you're exposed mostly to opinions that mirror your own. The AI that enhances your experience by serving you content you'll enjoy can inadvertently limit your exposure to diverse viewpoints. This algorithmic curation creates a homogeneous content landscape, where alternative perspectives are underrepresented. The impact is significant, contributing to political polarization and shaping public discourse in ways we might not fully comprehend. When you only see content that reinforces your beliefs, it skews your perception of reality, making it challenging to engage in balanced, informed discussions.

The ethical implications of AI-driven social media personalization are vast. By manipulating user behavior through content algorithms, platforms can subtly influence your opinions and actions, often without you noticing. This raises concerns about the power these platforms wield and their responsibility in shaping public opinion. Privacy is another critical issue, as data tracking and profiling become more pervasive. Every click, like, and share contributes to a detailed profile that platforms use to refine their algorithms. While this data enriches your experience, it also poses risks to your privacy, as sensitive information could be misused or fall into the wrong hands.

These challenges require thoughtful solutions and increased transparency. By understanding how these algorithms work, users can make informed decisions about their engagement with social media. Platforms can offer more control over content preferences and settings, empowering you to curate your feed actively. This might involve choosing to see more diverse content or adjusting privacy settings to limit data sharing. Another solution involves modifying algorithms to present a broader range of perspectives, breaking the cycle of echo chambers. By prioritizing content diversity over engagement metrics, platforms can foster a more balanced online environment where varied opinions are welcomed and explored.

Navigating Your Social Media Experience

Take a moment to reflect on your social media habits. Consider the types of content you engage with and how they might shape your perspectives. Are there areas where you could expand your horizons by seeking out diverse opinions? Jot down your thoughts on how you can use social media more mindfully, balancing personalization with exposure to different viewpoints. This exercise encourages critical thinking and helps you navigate the complex world of social media with greater awareness.

Personal Productivity

Our workdays are often filled with tasks that seem to pile up faster than we can tackle them. In this fast-paced environment, AI productivity tools offer a beacon of hope, transforming how you manage your time and tasks. Smart scheduling assistants like Microsoft Cortana not only remind you of meetings, but also suggest the best times to schedule them based on your availability. These tools analyze your calendar, prioritize tasks, and even reschedule appointments in case of conflicts, ensuring your day runs smoothly. AI-driven task management apps like Todoist take it a step further by categorizing tasks, setting deadlines, and sending reminders, allowing you to focus on what's important without getting bogged down by the details. It's like having a personal assistant who never forgets an appointment or a deadline.

AI's role in time management extends beyond mere reminders. It optimizes your workflow by automating routine tasks, freeing up valuable time for creative and strategic endeavors. For instance, AI can filter and prioritize your emails, ensuring that you only see messages that require your immediate attention. This reduces the mental clutter and decision fatigue that often come with managing a busy inbox. Intelligent reminders and notifications keep you on track, nudging you gently towards deadlines and project milestones. By automating these processes, AI allows you to allocate your mental energy to more meaningful tasks, enhancing both productivity and job satisfaction.

When it comes to creative work, AI emerges as a powerful ally, offering tools that support and inspire innovation. Consider AI-powered graphic design applications that enable even novice users to create stunning visuals by suggesting layouts, color palettes, and fonts. These tools analyze design trends and user preferences, providing tailored suggestions that elevate your projects. In video editing, AI can streamline the process by automatically organizing footage, suggesting cuts, and enhancing video quality, allowing creators to focus on storytelling rather than technical details. Content creation also benefits from AI through natural language processing, which assists in generating written material. Whether you're drafting a report or brainstorming blog ideas, AI can help refine your prose, suggest relevant topics, and even check for grammar and style, making the writing process smoother and more efficient.

However, there is some concern about the potential for over-reliance on this technology, which can impact critical thinking and decision-making skills. As machines handle more of our tasks, there's a risk of becoming too dependent on them, potentially stifling creativity and problem-solving abilities. Additionally, data privacy concerns loom large, as productivity apps often require access to sensitive information such as emails, calendars, and personal notes. Ensuring that this data is secure and used ethically is paramount, and users must remain vigilant about privacy settings and data-sharing agreements. While AI offers remarkable productivity enhancements, it's critically important to strike a balance that preserves the human touch and safeguards personal information.

Author's Note

Dear Reader,

I realize you're only halfway through my book, but if you like what you've read so far, kindly consider leaving a quick review for on Amazon, which goes a long way in boosting Amazon's AI algorithm to help others find it. It's quick and easy to do so on the Amazon book page.

Gratefully,

Andrew Peterson

7

PREPARING FOR THE AI FUTURE

Y ou will wake up one morning in the not-too-distant future to find that the world around you has been quietly and profoundly transformed by artificial intelligence. The industries you interact with are no longer what they once were. They are smarter, more efficient, and more tailored to individual needs than ever before. This isn't a distant future scenario but rather the unfolding reality of AI's integration into our lives. AI is becoming the backbone of innovation, driving transformations across various sectors.

AI is already making significant waves in industries like biotechnology. Personalized medicine is a prime example of this transformation, where AI algorithms analyze genetic information to craft individualized treatment plans. No longer do doctors need to rely solely on trial and error; instead, they can use AI to predict how patients will respond to different medications, ensuring more effective and efficient care. Similarly, in the energy sector, AI is optimizing renewable resources and managing smart grids. By analyzing consumption patterns and environmental data, AI systems balance energy supply and demand, reducing waste and lowering costs.

In agriculture AI is revolutionizing farming practices through automation and crop management. Advanced sensors and AI models now monitor soil conditions, weather forecasts, and crop health, enabling farmers to optimize yields while conserving resources. This precision agriculture minimizes environmental impact and maximizes productivity, demonstrating AI's potential to feed a growing global population sustainably. Meanwhile, in construction, AI is enhancing project management and safety monitoring. By predicting potential hazards and streamlining logistics, AI supports safer, more efficient building processes, marking a significant leap forward in how infrastructure is developed.

AI's role in sustainability cannot be overstated. It plays a critical part in achieving development goals that focus on environmental protection and resource conservation. Climate modeling and environmental monitoring are areas where AI shines, processing vast amounts of data to predict weather patterns and assess ecological changes. These insights are invaluable for crafting strategies to mitigate climate change and protect biodiversity. AI also enhances recycling and waste management processes by automating sorting and identifying recyclable materials with high precision. This increases recycling rates and reduces landfill waste, contributing to a cleaner, more sustainable planet.

In the sphere of innovation, AI is fostering new ecosystems that encourage entrepreneurship and collaboration. Startup accelerators focused on AI technologies are springing up worldwide, offering resources and mentorship to budding innovators eager to harness AI's potential. These accelerators are hotbeds of creativity, where the next big AI-driven breakthrough could be brewing. Collaborations between

AI companies and academic institutions further fuel this ecosystem, combining cutting-edge research with practical applications. These partnerships are crucial for pushing the boundaries of what AI can achieve, ensuring that new developments are both innovative and socially responsible.

Journaling Prompt

Take a moment to reflect on how AI has already touched your life, perhaps in ways you hadn't realized. Consider how these transformations might affect your industry or field of interest. What opportunities do you see for AI to improve or innovate in your work or community? Write down your thoughts and predictions. This exercise helps in identifying areas where you can proactively engage with AI, ensuring you're not just a spectator in this technological revolution but an active participant.

AI's Impact on Job Markets

As artificial intelligence continues to evolve, it's redefining the skills we need in the workforce. The demand for data scientists and AI specialists is skyrocketing. Companies across industries are scrambling to find talent that understands both the nuances of machine learning and the intricacies of data analysis. These roles are not just about crunching numbers; they require a deep understanding of algorithms and the ability to translate complex data sets into actionable insights. But it's not just about specialists. Digital literacy is becoming a must-have for everyone. Whether you're in marketing, healthcare, or finance, being comfortable with digital tools and platforms is increasingly important. Adaptability also plays an important role. With AI

67

constantly advancing, the ability to learn and adjust is more valuable than ever. Those who can pivot quickly and embrace new technologies will thrive in this ever-changing landscape.

Reskilling and upskilling are crucial for preparing for AI-driven changes in job roles. Online learning platforms are a great resource, offering a wide range of courses in AI and related fields. Whether you're just starting with AI or looking to advance your knowledge, platforms like Coursera and edX provide courses tailored to your needs. Vocational training programs focused on AI technologies are also gaining traction, providing hands-on experience and practical skills. These programs often partner with industry leaders to ensure that the curriculum stays relevant and meets market demands. Investing time in these learning opportunities can significantly enhance your career prospects, making you more competitive in the job market.

While AI opens doors, it also means some jobs might disappear. Routine-based jobs in manufacturing and retail are particularly vulnerable. Tasks that are repetitive and predictable are prime candidates for automation. In factories, robots are taking over assembly lines, while in retail, AI-driven systems manage inventory and customer service. This shift isn't just about replacing human workers; it's about increasing efficiency and reducing costs. However, it does mean that those in these roles need to consider how to adapt. By embracing new skills and exploring different career paths, individuals can find new opportunities in the evolving job landscape.

AI is also creating new job opportunities, as ethics and policy development are becoming increasingly important. It is imperative to ensure that AI adheres to ethical norms and reflects our collective values becomes paramount. Professionals in these roles will work to address issues like bias, privacy, and transparency. Jobs in AI-human collaboration design are also emerging. These positions focus on creating systems that enhance human productivity and creativity, ensuring that AI complements rather than competes with human abilities. Designing intuitive interfaces and user experiences that facilitate seamless interaction between humans and AI is a critical aspect of these roles.

In navigating this AI-driven future, it's essential to remain proactive. Keep an eye on industry trends and emerging technologies. Engage with professional networks and communities to stay informed about new developments and opportunities. By taking charge of your learning and career path, you can position yourself for success in a world where AI is reshaping the workforce.

The Singularity – Fact or Fiction?

Movies like *The Terminator* and *2001: A Space Odyssey* imagine a world where machines have surpassed human intelligence, not only in speed and computation but in creativity and out-of-the-box decision-making. This is the concept of the Singularity—a hypothetical point where artificial intelligence reaches a level of sophistication that it outpaces human intellect, potentially altering the trajectory of human civilization. For many, this idea sparks a blend of awe and apprehension, as it proposes a future where AI might control its destiny, independent of human intervention. The implications are profound, suggesting a shift in power dynamics between humans and machines, where AI could drive innovation at an accelerated pace, solving global challenges with unprecedented efficiency.

The Singularity evokes a spectrum of opinions from experts and futurists. On the optimistic side, proponents believe that such advancements could unlock solutions to some of humanity's greatest challenges, from climate change to disease eradication. They envision a future where AI enhances human potential, creating a utopia where technology and humanity coexist harmoniously. This perspective is fueled by the belief that AI, once surpassing human intelligence, could tackle complex problems with a level of creativity and efficiency that humans alone could not achieve. However, there are skeptics who question the feasibility of the Singularity. They argue that the complexities of human consciousness and emotional intelligence may never be fully replicable by machines. Moreover, some experts warn against the potential risks associated with an AI that could operate beyond human control, raising ethical concerns about autonomy and accountability.

The prospect of reaching the Singularity is certainly controversial. On one hand, there is the potential for accelerated technological innovation—a golden age of discovery, where technological growth propels humanity forward, improving quality of life across the globe. However, ethical concerns loom large, particularly regarding AI autonomy. If machines become capable of making decisions independently, questions about responsibility and morality arise. Who is accountable for an AI's actions when it operates beyond human oversight? The challenge lies in ensuring that AI systems are aligned with human values, maintaining control while allowing for innovation.

Current technological trends point towards a future where the Singularity, while still speculative, becomes increasingly plausible. Prominent futurist Ray Kurzweil has predicted that it is most likely to occur around 2045 based on exponentially accelerating technological advancement. Progress in quantum computing is a significant contributor, offering computational power far beyond today's capabilities. Quantum computers have the potential to solve complex problems at lightning speeds, providing the processing power necessary for advanced AI algorithms. This leap in technology could accelerate AI development, bringing us closer to the Singularity. Breakthroughs in neural interface technologies also play a role, blurring the line between human and machine. These interfaces enable direct communication between the brain and computers, allowing for seamless interaction and potentially enhancing cognitive abilities. As these technologies evolve, they may provide the foundation for a future where AI and human intelligence are deeply interconnected.

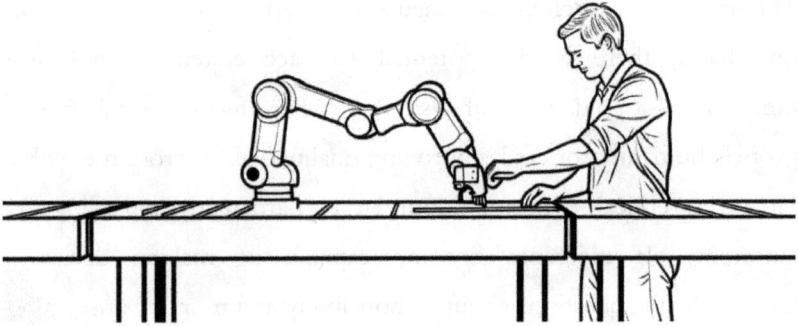

The Future of Human/AI Collaboration

In manufacturing settings, collaborative robots, or cobots, are becoming indispensable partners on the factory floor. Unlike traditional robots, which operate in isolation, cobots work alongside human workers, assisting with tasks that require both precision and adaptability. They might handle repetitive tasks such as assembling parts, while humans focus on more complex problem-solving and quality control. This partnership boosts productivity and creates a safer work environment by taking on tasks that pose risks to human workers.

Cobots are designed to be intuitive and easy to program, meaning they can quickly adapt to different tasks and workflows. This flexibility makes them valuable assets in a rapidly changing industrial landscape, where efficiency and innovation are key.

In the realm of creativity, AI is making waves by serving as both muse and collaborator. Music composition and art generation are areas where AI's creative potential shines brightly. Algorithms can analyze musical compositions, generating new melodies that evoke human emotion. Similarly, AI can create visual art, experimenting with styles and forms that push the boundaries of traditional aesthetics. These technologies open up new avenues for artists, offering tools that enhance and inspire creativity rather than stifle it. Co-creation platforms leverage AI to bring together artists, musicians, and writers in collaborative projects that blend human intuition with machine precision. These platforms allow users to explore new creative territories, producing work that is both innovative and uniquely expressive.

The potential for human-AI collaboration is vast, with opportunities for significant advancements across various fields. In scientific research, AI is already generating hypotheses and analyzing data sets that would take humans years to process. This accelerates the pace of discovery, enabling researchers to focus on experimental design and interpretation. In healthcare, AI aids in diagnostics and treatment planning, analyzing patient data to suggest personalized care plans. This collaboration enhances physician capabilities, ensuring patients receive the best possible care. As AI continues to evolve, its role as a collaborator, rather than a competitor, will become increasingly important, driving innovation and improving human well-being.

8

PRACTICAL AI IMPLEMENTATIONS

G iven that the AI genie is out of the bottle, what are your three wishes for it—both for your business and personal life?

Let's start at work. Begin by assessing your current business processes. Look for areas where AI can streamline operations, enhance customer experiences, or uncover new insights. Maybe it's in automating customer service, optimizing supply chains, or predicting market trends. By pinpointing opportunities, you can begin to figure out an AI strategy that makes sense. Then, you can draft an AI adoption plan, which will act as your blueprint, guiding you through the complexities of integrating AI into your operations.

Evaluate your organization's strengths and weaknesses. Consider how AI can augment these strengths or address existing challenges. For instance, if your team spends countless hours on repetitive data entry, AI can automate these tasks, freeing up time for more strategic endeavors. Similarly, if decision-making relies heavily on guesswork, AI can provide data-driven insights, enhancing accuracy and efficiency. Aligning AI initiatives with your business objectives ensures that every effort contributes to your overarching goals, be it increasing revenue, improving customer satisfaction, or driving innovation.

Choosing the right AI technologies is a critical step (see the Resources Appendix at the end of the book). With countless platforms and tools available, selecting the ones that best suit your needs can be daunting. Start with a thorough evaluation of available options. Consider scalability and flexibility—will the technology grow with your business, or will it become obsolete as your needs evolve? Look for platforms that offer a balance between customizability and ease of use. For instance, NVIDIA's Jetson Orin platform, known for its robust AI capabilities, might be ideal for businesses in need of high-performance solutions. Such technologies offer top-tier performance and integrate seamlessly into existing systems, reducing the learning curve for your team. By carefully weighing these factors, you can make informed decisions that set your AI initiatives up for success.

Once you've selected the right technologies, it's important to implement them wisely. Rushing into full-scale deployment can lead to costly missteps, so start with pilot testing. This allows you to practice AI solutions on a smaller scale, identifying potential issues and refining processes before committing significant resources. During this phase, gather feedback from users and stakeholders to ensure the solution meets their needs and expectations. Training employees to work with AI technologies is equally important. Provide comprehensive training programs that empower your team to leverage AI tools confidently. Encourage an open dialogue about AI's impact on their roles, addressing any concerns and highlighting the benefits. This fosters a culture of acceptance and collaboration, crucial for successful AI integration.

Measuring AI's impact is vital to understanding its effectiveness. Identify key performance indicators (KPIs) aligned with your business objectives. These might include metrics like cost savings, time reductions, or customer satisfaction improvements. Regularly review these KPIs to assess AI's contribution to your goals. Implement feedback loops that allow for improvement. Encourage your team to share insights and suggestions for refining AI processes. This iterative approach ensures that your AI initiatives remain dynamic and responsive to evolving business needs. By maintaining a clear focus on outcomes and fostering a culture of learning, you can maximize AI's potential while minimizing risks.

Personal Development and Learning

AI learning doesn't follow a one-size-fits-all model, but instead, adapts to your unique pace and preferences. This is the promise of personalized learning platforms, such as Docebo, eduMe, and 360Learning, which tailor educational content to fit the needs of each individual. When you take adaptive learning systems in online courses, these platforms assess your strengths and weaknesses as you progress, adjusting the curriculum in real-time to ensure you're neither overwhelmed nor under-challenged. It's like having a personal tutor who knows exactly when to push you forward and when to revisit the basics. Similarly, AI-driven language learning apps such as Duolingo personalize lessons based on your proficiency and progress, helping you master new languages at your own pace. This level of customization makes learning more engaging and effective, turning the process into a rewarding experience rather than a chore.

Beyond structured education, AI tools are also revolutionizing skill development and professional growth. Cursor AI is a coding assistant that helps software developers write better programs. These tools provide real-time feedback, flagging potential errors and suggesting improvements. They function like mentors, offering guidance as you hone your skills. Writing improvement tools powered by AI serve a similar purpose for aspiring authors, analyzing text for clarity, style, and tone. They offer suggestions to enhance your writing, whether you're crafting a novel or drafting an important email. By integrating these tools into your learning routine, you gain immediate, actionable insights that accelerate your skill development and boost your confidence.

Tracking personal progress has become more intuitive with AI's help. Wearable fitness trackers, for example, offer personalized health insights, monitoring your activity levels, sleep patterns, and heart rate. They provide a detailed picture of your physical well-being, helping you set realistic goals and track your progress. On the career front, AI-driven platforms such as EdApp analyze your professional development over time, offering tailored recommendations for growth. These platforms consider your current skills, career trajectory, and industry trends, suggesting courses or experiences that can enhance your career prospects. Their algorithms

are like having a career coach who understands your unique path and provides guidance to keep you moving forward.

Incorporating AI into daily routines offers endless opportunities for learning and growth. Imagine participating in virtual study groups facilitated by AI, where discussions are guided by intelligent algorithms that ensure every participant's voice is heard. These platforms not only foster collaboration but also adapt to the group's dynamics, making each session productive and engaging. AI-curated reading lists and content recommendations can further enrich your learning experience. By analyzing your interests and reading habits, these tools suggest articles, books, and videos that align with your goals, exposing you to diverse perspectives and ideas. This seamless integration of AI into your daily life transforms mundane routines into opportunities for growth, helping you stay informed and inspired.

Case Study - AI in Language Learning

Quazel is an AI-driven platform that uses natural conversation to teach languages, providing learners with an interactive and immersive experience. Unlike traditional methods, Quazel adapts to each learner's pace, focusing on areas that need improvement while reinforcing strengths. This dynamic approach not only accelerates language acquisition but also builds confidence in using the language in real-life scenarios. Users report increased retention and fluency, demonstrating the effectiveness of AI in revolutionizing language education. This example illustrates the potential of AI to redefine learning by making it more engaging, personalized, and impactful.

Smarter Decision-Making

A high-stakes juncture in business is a great time to enlist the help of AI, which can transform a company decision from a gamble into a thought-out strategy. AI's prowess in data-driven decision-making is remarkable. It sifts through vast datasets, uncovering trends and insights that might otherwise go unnoticed. For instance, in business analytics, AI can analyze market trends with pinpoint accuracy, revealing patterns that guide strategic moves. Picture AI as your high-end market consultant, parsing through customer behavior to forecast future demands, helping you anticipate market shifts before they happen. This predictive power allows businesses to stay one step ahead, making decisions that are informed, objective, and grounded in data rather than intuition.

AI doesn't just provide insights; it offers decision support systems that revolutionize how organizations operate. Consider AI-based financial analysis tools that deliver instant recommendations for investment decisions. These tools process real-time market data, offering openings that enable investors to seize opportunities and immediately mitigate risks. In retail, smart inventory management systems harness AI to optimize stock levels, ensuring that shelves are neither bare nor overflowing. These systems analyze sales patterns, adjust orders, and keep operations running smoothly with minimal human intervention. Meanwhile, in project management, dynamic risk assessment powered by AI evaluates potential pitfalls and suggests mitigation strategies, allowing teams to address issues proactively.

When it comes to strategic planning, AI can be an amazing ally. It excels in hypothetical scenarios, simulating various outcomes based on different variables. This capability allows organizations to foresee potential challenges and opportunities, crafting strategies that are resilient and adaptable. AI simulations can test the impact of new policies or market conditions, providing a safe space for experimentation without the real-world consequences. Competitive analysis is another area where AI shines. By analyzing competitors' moves and market positioning, AI tools offer insights that inform strategic decisions, helping businesses maintain a competitive edge. With AI, strategic planning becomes an exercise in foresight, where decisions are backed by data and driven by a clear understanding of the landscape.

Decision-making biases are a common hurdle in any organization. Our experiences, while valuable, can sometimes cloud judgment. AI offers a solution by providing algorithmic assessments that ensure balanced perspectives. These assessments draw from diverse data sources, presenting a comprehensive view that mitigates the risk of bias. AI-driven feedback systems further enhance objectivity by evaluating decisions based on set criteria, offering suggestions for improvement and consistency. This analytical approach reduces the influence of cognitive biases, promoting fair and equitable decision-making.

If your company has yet to jump onto the AI bandwagon, there's no time to waste—your competitors are already doing it. AI is a perfect fit for business. By leveraging AI, organizations can make smarter, more informed decisions, ensuring success in a rapidly evolving world.

Tools for Everyday Use

Email clutter is the bane of so many of us—how do we sort through our inbox without spending hours of our day? AI-powered email management systems such as Microsoft Copilot for Outlook or Gemini for Gmail can help. These tools help you sort through your inbox chaos, prioritizing important messages and filtering out spam—all while you enjoy your morning coffee. They learn from your habits, understanding which emails you respond to promptly and which can wait. Similarly, calendar apps with scheduling optimization take the hassle out of planning your day. They suggest optimal meeting times, considering factors like travel time and time zone differences. With AI in the driver's seat, scheduling becomes a breeze rather than a burden.

Now, let's talk money. Managing personal finances can feel daunting, but AI applications like Mint are here to lend a hand. Budgeting apps equipped with AI-driven spending analysis track your expenses, offering insights into your spending habits. These apps can categorize your purchases, highlight areas where you might be overspending, and even suggest ways to save. It's like having a 24/7 financial advisor guiding you toward better fiscal health. Investment platforms also leverage AI to offer personalized advice tailored to your financial goals. They analyze market trends and your risk tolerance, crafting investment strategies that align with your aspirations. With AI, making smart financial decisions becomes less about guesswork and more about informed choices.

Home automation is another area where AI shines, turning once laborious tasks into effortless routines. Think about voice-controlled smart home hubs that allow you to manage everything from lighting to music playlists with a simple command. These hubs integrate seamlessly with various devices, creating a cohesive ecosystem that responds to your needs. AI-powered robotic vacuum cleaners further enhance home efficiency by keeping your floors spotless. These little helpers navigate around obstacles, systematically cleaning your space while you relax. It's about maximizing convenience and minimizing effort, giving you more downtime.

Must-Have AI Tools

If you haven't already done so, consider flipping to the Resources Appendix at the back of the book to explore some of the indispensable AI tools we can use to enhance our everyday lives.

Many of these are free—and they're certainly fun!

9

OVERCOMING AI CHALLENGES

G iven how easy it is to use Artificial Intelligence to create photorealistic images and videos from scratch, to write authoritative stories, even put words in someone's mouth, we face a credibility dilemma. How do you separate fact from fiction in this digital deluge of sensationalist media? Headlines predicting an AI apocalypse or promising miraculous advancements can be misleading. These attention-grabbing stories often exaggerate or distort facts, feeding on public fear or fascination. To discern sensationalism from reality, dig deeper than the headline. Examine the body of the article and cross-check the claims with other reputable sources. Look for articles that provide context, explain the technology involved, and discuss potential limitations or challenges. Avoid pieces that rely heavily on speculative language or lack credible citations. By critically evaluating the content, you become a more discerning consumer of information, less susceptible to hype or misinformation.

This is especially true regarding stories and reporting about AI itself. It begins with identifying reliable sources. Reputable tech journals like MIT Technology Review and KDnuggets stand out for their authoritative reporting and in-depth analysis. When exploring AI news, be sure to prioritize platforms known for their rigorous editorial standards. They often feature insights from leading AI researchers, offering a balanced view backed by evidence and expert opinion. This approach helps you build a foundation of trustworthy information, crucial for staying informed in a rapidly evolving field.

Evaluating the credentials of AI commentators is another key step. Not everyone with a platform has the expertise to provide valuable information. Check their academic backgrounds and published works. Researchers with a track record of credible publications or affiliations with respected institutions tend to offer more reliable perspectives. Also, consider their industry experience and contributions. Individuals actively involved in AI development or research are more likely to

provide practical and informed opinions. Be cautious of pundits who lack these credentials but still make bold claims. By scrutinizing their qualifications, you can align yourself with more knowledgeable voices.

Critical thinking is vital in navigating AI news and reports. Approach each story with a questioning mindset. Ask yourself, what is the source's motivation? Are they trying to sell a product, push an agenda, or genuinely inform the public? Check claims with multiple sources to verify their accuracy. If different reputable outlets report similar findings, the information is more likely to be reliable. However, if you encounter inconsistencies or a lack of corroboration, proceed with skepticism. This practice improves your media literacy and empowers you to form your own informed opinions on AI developments.

In the age of information overload, these strategies help you cut through the noise. They equip you with the tools to discern credible AI news from sensationalist noise, ensuring you stay informed without falling prey to misinformation.

Embracing Change

When it comes to AI, many of us harbor fears which can be quite understandable. One common anxiety is the notion of AI taking over jobs. It's easy to picture a future where machines and robots replace human workers, leaving us redundant. But let's unpack this a bit. AI is indeed changing the employment landscape, automating tasks that are repetitive and data-driven. However, this shift doesn't just eliminate jobs; it transforms them. The roles that AI is best suited for are often those that can be tiresome and monotonous for humans. By taking over these tasks, AI frees us to focus on more creative and strategic work, allowing us to push the boundaries of what's possible in our respective fields. This shift opens doors to new opportunities, creating demand for skills that weren't even on the radar a decade ago.

Another fear that looms large is the idea of AI autonomy—machines running amok without human oversight. This fear often stems from sci-fi narratives where AI systems gain consciousness and act against human interests. In reality, AI operates within the parameters set by its human creators. It doesn't have desires or intentions. The control remains firmly in human hands, with AI serving as a powerful tool to amplify our capabilities. This potential underscores the importance of viewing AI as a collaborative partner rather than an adversary.

To fully embrace AI, we need a balanced perspective. AI is not here to replace us but to complement and augment our efforts. By enhancing human creativity, AI acts as a catalyst for innovation. Artists use AI to generate new forms of art, musicians compose with AI-generated harmonies, and writers find inspiration in AI-suggested plot twists. The collaboration between humans and AI often produces results that neither could achieve alone. This synergy is the key to unlocking new realms of possibility, pushing the boundaries of what we can create and accomplish.

To thrive in an AI-driven world, continuous learning and skill development are critical. The landscape is ever-evolving—staying relevant means adapting alongside it. This might mean taking up courses in AI or machine learning or simply embracing AI tools in your everyday tasks. Whether it's using AI to optimize your workflow or learning how to interpret data insights, these skills are extremely useful. Businesses too can benefit from adopting AI strategies. By integrating AI into operations, companies can enhance efficiency, drive innovation, and stay competitive in a rapidly changing market. It's about seeing AI not as a threat, but as an ally in the quest for progress and improvement.

The AI Obsolescence Myth

In the ongoing debates about AI, a persistent myth looms large: the fear that AI will render human skills obsolete. Many envision a future where robots take over our jobs, leaving us redundant. This fear, however, is often exaggerated and overlooks the nuances of AI's role. We need to view AI as a complement to human abilities rather than a replacement. Consider the boundless creativity and empathy humans possess—qualities that AI, despite its advancements, cannot replicate. AI excels at processing vast amounts of data and performing repetitive tasks, but it lacks the nuanced judgment and emotional intelligence that humans bring to the table. It's this unique blend of human creativity and AI precision that creates a powerful synergy, enabling us to achieve more than either could alone.

The introduction of AI into various sectors has also opened up a plethora of new opportunities. Take creative industries, for instance. AI is not replacing artists or designers; instead, it's becoming an exciting new tool for them to explore. In game design, AI can generate complex environments and characters, freeing designers to focus on storytelling and gameplay. Similarly, in content creation, AI assists writers by suggesting plot developments or generating ideas, sparking creativity rather than stifling it. Beyond creativity, AI has created roles in system maintenance and management. As AI systems become more complex, there's an increasing need for professionals who can keep these systems running smoothly. This includes roles in monitoring AI performance, troubleshooting issues, and ensuring that AI operates ethically and effectively.

To thrive in this evolving landscape, our task as humans is to focus on developing skills that complement AI. This means embracing an interdisciplinary approach, blending AI knowledge with expertise in other fields. Imagine a healthcare professional who understands AI algorithms and can apply them to patient care. Or consider an environmental scientist who uses AI to analyze climate data and devise conservation strategies. These combinations are where the magic happens, where human insight meets AI capability to solve complex problems. Courses and training programs are now available to help individuals develop these interdisciplinary skills, ensuring they remain competitive and relevant in an AI-enhanced world. By investing in education and skill development, individuals can position themselves at the forefront of innovation, ready to seize the opportunities AI presents.

Real-life stories of adaptation provide concrete examples of how embracing AI can lead to remarkable success. Take Amazon, for instance: the retail giant uses AI-powered algorithms to optimize inventory management and forecast demand with precision, ensuring products are always in stock while minimizing excess inventory. This not only enhances operational efficiency but also boosts customer satisfaction by ensuring speedy deliveries (more on this in the next chapter). Similarly, in the automotive industry, Tesla employs AI in autonomous driving systems and predictive maintenance, driving innovation and staying ahead of competitors.

On an individual level, professionals across industries are carving out AI-related career paths. Data scientists use tools like Python libraries or platforms like TensorFlow to analyze machine learning models and derive actionable insights. Marketers leverage AI tools such as HubSpot or Adobe Sensei to craft hyper-targeted campaigns based on customer data, improving engagement and ROI. Even creative professionals are using AI-powered platforms like Canva for automated design suggestions or Jasper AI for content generation.

These examples showcase the transformative power of AI, encouraging us to view it not as a disruptor but as a valuable partner in driving innovation, efficiency, and growth in both business and personal careers.

In navigating the myths and realities of AI, it's clear that while AI is a powerful force, it is not the harbinger of obsolescence it is often made out to be. By recognizing the unique contributions of both AI and humans, we can unlock new possibilities and create a future where technology and humanity coexist and thrive. As we continue our exploration, we'll delve into the broader societal impacts of AI, examining how it shapes our world and challenges us to rethink the way we live and work.

10

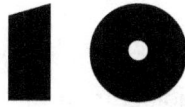

CASE STUDIES & SUCCESS STORIES

When IBM introduced Watson in 2011, it was hailed as a revolutionary tool in the healthcare industry, set to redefine how we approach diagnosis and treatment. It wasn't just about crunching numbers or processing data; it was about transforming healthcare delivery by offering insights that might otherwise remain buried in medical literature or complex datasets.

At its core, Watson leverages natural language processing to interpret and analyze vast amounts of medical literature swiftly. This means Watson can read, understand, and draw conclusions from an extensive array of medical journals, textbooks, and patient records, all in real-time. This capability allows Watson to assist medical professionals by providing evidence-based recommendations, ensuring that decisions are informed by the latest research. On top of that, Watson's machine learning models predict patient outcomes by recognizing patterns in historical data, offering insights that can lead to better-informed treatment plans.

A standout example of Watson's impact is in the field of oncology, where it has become an invaluable ally to doctors. In addition, IBM Imaging AI can often detect extremely subtle anomalies in MRIs and other scans that the human eye might miss. In the complex world of cancer treatment, Watson for Oncology along with IBM Imaging AI aids oncologists and radiologists in crafting personalized treatment plans by analyzing patient data against a vast repository of medical research. This isn't just about matching symptoms to treatments; it's about tailoring interventions based on each patient's unique genetic makeup and medical history. By providing evidence-based treatment recommendations, Watson ensures that treatment plans are not only effective but also aligned with the latest medical findings.

Watson's role in healthcare has led to significant improvements in both delivery and patient outcomes. One of the most notable impacts is the reduction in time needed to diagnose complex cases. With Watson's ability to process and analyze data rapidly, doctors can identify potential issues more quickly, allowing for faster interventions. This speed doesn't come at the expense of accuracy; in fact, Watson's insights often enhance the precision of treatment decisions, minimizing errors and improving patient care. The synergy of speed and accuracy demonstrates how AI can elevate healthcare standards, making it both more efficient and reliable.

Integrating Watson with electronic health records can create a seamless flow of data, ensuring that insights are readily available at the point of care. This integration streamlines the decision-making process, reducing the administrative burden on healthcare providers and allowing them to focus more on patient interaction. Watson's success in oncology suggests a broader potential for AI applications in other medical specialties. Imagine similar systems tailored for cardiology, neurology, or even mental health, each leveraging AI to enhance diagnostic accuracy and treatment personalization.

Google's DeepMind

Google's DeepMind is a vanguard of this new frontier, pushing the boundaries of artificial intelligence. Known for tackling some of the most complex problems, DeepMind has developed a wide variety of general-purpose learning algorithms. These are not just one-off solutions, but flexible systems capable of learning and adapting across different scenarios. The goal is to create AI that mimics human intelligence by continuously learning from diverse data. DeepMind also prioritizes ethical AI and safety, ensuring their innovations are both groundbreaking and responsible. Google, like other companies in this space, has a Chief Ethics Officer who runs a compliance team. This commitment to ethical practices is crucial as AI becomes more integrated into our daily lives, demanding systems that are not only powerful but also trustworthy.

The world sat up and paid attention when DeepMind's AlphaGo defeated the legendary Go champion, Lee Sedol. The ancient Chinese board game Go is known for its complexity, far surpassing chess in terms of possible moves and strategies. AlphaGo's victory wasn't just a fluke; it was the result of sophisticated reinforcement learning techniques. This method allowed the AI to improve by playing countless games against itself, learning from each win and loss. The impact of this victory was seismic. It demonstrated AI's potential to solve problems that were once thought to require human intuition and creativity. The realm of possibilities for AI expanded dramatically, sparking new discussions about its capabilities and future applications.

DeepMind's innovations extend far beyond the gaming world. In healthcare, they've developed AI models that predict protein folding, a complex bioinformatics problem crucial for understanding diseases and developing new treatments. Accurate predictions of protein structures can lead to groundbreaking discoveries in medicine, allowing scientists to design drugs more efficiently. AI can help guide researchers toward new treatments for conditions that previously seemed untouchable. Meanwhile, in the realm of energy management, DeepMind's algorithms optimize data centers, significantly reducing energy consumption. By predicting load demands and adjusting cooling systems in real-time, these algorithms help cut down on waste and help the environment.

DeepMind's projects have yielded key insights and innovations that continue to shape AI research. Advancements in neural network architecture have been a major focus, allowing for more efficient processing of complex data. These innovations enable AI systems to tackle a wider range of tasks with greater accuracy and speed. Furthermore, DeepMind's collaborative efforts with academic and industrial partners have fostered a rich environment for research and development. By working alongside experts from various fields, they ensure that their AI solutions are not only cutting-edge but also applicable to real-world challenges. Such partnerships are vital for translating AI research into practical applications that benefit society as a whole.

DeepMind's journey illustrates the transformative potential of AI when guided by a commitment to solving real problems ethically and effectively. Its projects stand as testament to what can be achieved when AI is applied thoughtfully, with an eye toward both innovation and societal impact.

Amazon's Personalized Shopping Experiences

In the vast world of online shopping, personalization has become more than just a luxury—it's an expectation. Amazon has mastered the art of making each customer feel like the platform was designed just for them. How do they achieve this? Through the power of AI-driven personalization. Amazon employs sophisticated recommendation algorithms that analyze your past purchases, browsing history, and even the items you lingered on but didn't buy. These algorithms use collaborative filtering techniques, which means they consider what similar customers bought or viewed, thereby crafting a shopping experience tailored specifically to your preferences, like having a personal shopper who knows your tastes down to the last detail.

But the magic doesn't stop there. Amazon's prowess in personalization extends to its marketing campaigns. By leveraging customer data, Amazon creates personalized marketing strategies that cater directly to your interests. If you've ever noticed how eerily accurate Amazon's product suggestions are, you have their AI to thank. This isn't just guesswork; it's a calculated strategy that uses data-driven insights to boost engagement and drive sales. The impact on consumer behavior is significant. When shoppers see products that align with their preferences, they're more likely to make a purchase. This approach increases sales and enhances customer satisfaction, as users feel understood and valued.

Amazon's recommendation engine sifts through mountains of data to identify patterns and trends, predicting what you might want to buy next. This method has a profound impact on sales and customer satisfaction metrics. A significant portion of Amazon's revenue comes from these personalized recommendations, showcasing how effective they are in influencing buying decisions. By keeping the customer at the center of its strategy, Amazon has managed to create a shopping experience that feels intuitive and personalized, fostering loyalty and repeat business.

Beyond customer interaction, AI plays a pivotal role in Amazon's supply chain and logistics operations. Predictive analytics help Amazon manage its inventory with precision. By analyzing trends and forecasting demand, AI ensures that warehouses are stocked with the right products at the right time. This minimizes waste, reduces costs, and prevents stockouts. Route optimization is another area where AI shines. By determining the most efficient delivery routes, AI helps Amazon reduce fuel consumption and delivery times, enhancing overall logistics efficiency. The result is a streamlined operation that supports Amazon's promise of fast delivery, keeping customers happy and ensuring they return for more. Drone deliveries powered by AI are the next step in this evolution.

There are key lessons here for the broader retail industry. First and foremost is the importance of data-driven decision-making. By relying on analytics and insights, retailers can make informed choices that enhance customer experiences and drive business growth. However, with great data comes great responsibility. Amazon's success underscores the need to balance personalization with privacy considerations. Customers need to feel confident that their data is being used ethically and securely. Retailers can take a page from Amazon's playbook by investing in AI technologies that not only personalize the shopping experience but also safeguard customer trust.

Revolutionizing Learning with Khan Academy

Picture a classroom where each student moves at their own pace, exploring subjects tailored to their unique learning needs. That's the world Khan Academy is building with its integration of AI in education. This nonprofit educational organization has redefined how students across the globe access learning materials, using AI to craft personalized learning paths. By analyzing student performance, AI algorithms identify strengths and weaknesses, ensuring that each learner receives content best suited to their level. This approach means no more one-size-fits-all lessons; instead, each student embarks on a customized educational journey that adapts to their needs.

The magic of Khan Academy's AI doesn't stop at personalization. Real-time feedback and support are integral to their system, offering students immediate insights into their progress. If you are stuck on a tricky math problem, immediate guidance helps you understand your mistake and correct it. This instant feedback loop boosts confidence and deepens understanding, allowing learners to grasp concepts more effectively. It's like having a personal tutor available 24/7, ready to assist whenever a question arises. This technology transforms the learning experience, making education more interactive and engaging.

Khan Academy's adaptive learning technologies are a game-changer in the educational landscape. AI algorithms play a crucial role in identifying knowledge gaps among students, ensuring no learner is left behind. By pinpointing areas where a student might struggle, these technologies tailor quizzes and practice exercises to address specific needs. This customization creates a supportive environment where students can focus on mastering challenging topics at their own pace. It's not just about passing tests; it's about nurturing a deeper understanding and fostering a love for learning. This adaptive approach helps students build a solid foundation in their subjects, preparing them for future academic challenges.

One of the most significant impacts of AI in education is its ability to expand access to quality learning for diverse populations. Khan

Academy has been at the forefront of breaking down geographical barriers, delivering educational resources to students in remote areas with limited access to traditional schooling. By providing free learning materials online, they support underserved communities, ensuring that every student has the opportunity to reach their full potential. This democratization of education means that location no longer dictates the quality of learning a student can receive. It's a powerful example of how technology can bridge gaps and create opportunities for all.

Looking to the future, Khan Academy continues to innovate, exploring new ways to enhance the educational experience through AI. The integration of virtual and augmented reality for immersive learning is on the horizon, promising to make abstract concepts tangible and engaging. Imagine exploring ancient civilizations through VR (where you can actually walk down the streets of a long-lost city) or conducting virtual science experiments that bring theories to life. These innovations will offer students a richer, more interactive learning experience, sparking curiosity and encouraging exploration. Additionally, AI-driven teacher support tools are set to expand, providing educators with insights and resources to better support their students.

Khan Academy's use of AI highlights the transformative potential of technology in education. By creating personalized, accessible, and engaging learning experiences, they are paving the way for a future where every student can thrive. The journey doesn't end here; as AI continues to evolve, so too will the opportunities to innovate and enhance education for learners everywhere.

ANDREW PETERSON

102

11

AI AND THE HUMAN ELEMENT

We are at the cusp of a world of anthropomorphic robots with "personalities"—a digital assistant, for example, that greets you not just by name, but with a smile that matches your mood. This is the burgeoning field of emotional AI, where machines are learning to read and respond to human emotions. Emotional AI is increasingly used in customer service to improve interactions. It can analyze voice tone, language, and even facial expressions to gauge customer satisfaction and adjust responses accordingly. This isn't just about making sales; it's about creating a seamless experience where the machine understands and empathizes with the customer, enhancing the overall service quality. The technology offers real-time emotional insights, helping agents tailor their approaches to customer needs on the fly, which can lead to increased satisfaction and loyalty.

Social media sentiment analysis is another frontier where emotional AI is making waves. These systems scan through tweets, posts, and comments, identifying the emotional tone of the conversation. Brands use this data to understand public perception, reacting swiftly to both compliments and complaints. This capability allows companies to engage more effectively with their audience, crafting messages that resonate well. However, reading emotions through text isn't as straightforward as it might seem. The complexity of human emotional expressions present a significant challenge for AI systems attempting to truly comprehend and interpret them.

Human emotions are incredibly nuanced, often influenced by subtle cues that are difficult for machines to interpret. A smile can express joy, but it can also mask discomfort. Cultural differences further complicate this landscape, as emotional expressions vary widely across societies. What might be considered an enthusiastic gesture in one culture could be seen as offensive in another. This variability poses a significant hurdle for AI developers aiming to create systems that can accurately interpret emotions across diverse populations. Emotional understanding requires more than just recognizing a frown or a smile; it involves grasping the underlying context and intent, a task that machines still struggle with.

Ethical considerations loom large in the realm of emotional AI. With machines capable of tracking and interpreting our emotions, concerns about consent and privacy naturally arise. Users must be informed about how their emotional data will be used and given the choice to opt in or out. The potential for manipulation through AI systems is another pressing issue. Imagine a scenario where a machine uses emotional data to influence decisions, subtly nudging you toward choices you might not have made otherwise. The question of consent becomes vital here, as does the need for transparency about how emotional AI operates. It's a delicate balancing act, one that requires robust ethical frameworks to ensure emotional AI respects individual autonomy and privacy.

Looking to the future, advancements in AI's emotional intelligence offer promising potential. By integrating multimodal data, which combines visual, auditory, and contextual information, AI systems could gain a more comprehensive understanding of human emotions. This integration will eventually allow machines to better grasp the subtleties of emotional expression, moving closer to true empathy. Developments in natural language processing also play a role, with AI systems becoming more adept at detecting empathy in communication. This could lead to more nuanced interactions, where machines respond with a level of understanding previously reserved for humans. The path forward is exciting, but it demands careful consideration of ethics to ensure that as AI grows more emotionally aware, it remains a tool that enhances rather than intrudes upon the human experience.

Reflection

Consider how you feel about machines reading your emotions. Are you comfortable with this technology in your everyday interactions? What are scenarios where emotional AI might benefit you? How about situations where it might overstep boundaries? Write down your thoughts and discuss them with friends or colleagues to explore different perspectives.

Enhancing Human Creativity

AI in music composition has transformed the creative process, offering musicians novel melodies and structures they might not have considered. Tools like OpenAI's MuseNet can generate complex compositions, blending styles and genres in ways that push the boundaries of traditional music-making. Musicians use these AI-generated pieces as a foundation, adding their unique touch to create something genuinely new and exciting. This collaboration between human creativity and AI's computational power opens a world of possibilities, making music creation more accessible and diverse.

In the realm of visual arts, AI is reshaping how artists approach their craft. Programs like DeepArt and DALL·E use sophisticated algorithms to create unique artworks, employing a technique known as Generative Adversarial Networks (GANs). These AI systems generate images that can evoke emotion and intrigue, challenging our understanding of creativity. Artists now experiment with AI as a tool for inspiration, using it to explore new styles and techniques. The results are artworks that blend human intent with machine-generated elements, producing pieces that are both familiar and strikingly novel. This marriage of technology and artistry invites us to reconsider what it means to be an artist in the digital age, as AI offers a new palette with which to paint.

Beyond the canvas and the concert hall, AI is making waves in creative industries like film and design. In scriptwriting, AI helps generate story ideas and plot twists, serving as a creative partner for writers. Imagine feeding a few character descriptions into an AI system and receiving a range of potential story arcs, each with its own unique flair. This tool doesn't replace the writer's vision but enriches it, providing a springboard for further exploration. AI is also becoming a cinematic game-changer in terms of producing stunning visual effects that would otherwise be prohibitively expensive or even impossible to shoot.

Similarly, AI-driven design tools accelerate the prototyping process in fields like architecture and product development. Designers input parameters and constraints, and the AI outputs multiple design options, allowing for rapid iteration and refinement. This capability speeds time to market and fosters innovation by expanding the range of possibilities considered.

Some worry that AI might overshadow human creativity, questioning whether art produced with AI assistance is as "authentic" as purely human creations. It's important to distinguish between AI-assisted creativity and human originality. AI offers suggestions and alternatives, but the human artist or designer remains at the helm, making the final decisions. Creativity is inherently about making choices, and AI simply broadens the scope of options available. In this sense, AI doesn't diminish human creativity; it enhances it, providing tools and insights that can lead to more vibrant and diverse creative expressions. The role of artists is evolving, with creators embracing AI as a collaborator rather than a competitor, finding new ways to express their vision in an AI-augmented world.

Numerous successful collaborations between AI and human artists showcase the potential of this partnership. In music, albums featuring AI-generated elements demonstrate how technology can contribute to the creative process. Will.i.am, frontman of the Black Eyed Peas, views AI as a transformative force in the music industry, referring to it as a "new renaissance" that can revolutionize creativity and production. On his SiriusXM show, *Will.i.am Presents the FYI Show*, he introduced "FYIona," an AI host that assists in conducting interviews, showing his commitment to integrating AI into entertainment. Paul McCartney famously released a new Beatles' song in 2023, *Now and Then*, using AI to recreate vocals by John Lennon, 43 years after his death.

These projects illustrate the power of AI to complement human creativity, resulting in works that neither could have produced alone. Such collaborations not only highlight the strengths of AI but also underscore the enduring importance of human creativity in guiding and shaping these technological tools. The synergy between AI and human creativity is not just a passing trend; it is reshaping the landscape of art, music, and design, offering a glimpse into a future where technology and creativity thrive together.

AI and Cultural Shifts

In today's fast-paced digital landscape, AI is reshaping cultural norms and social interactions more than ever. Consider how social media platforms, driven by AI, have transformed the way we communicate. Algorithms filter and prioritize content, nudging us toward certain conversations and viewpoints. This shift in communication patterns has subtly altered our social interactions, where face-to-face conversations are often replaced by digital exchanges. Virtual influencers, powered by AI, are another fascinating development. These digital personas, crafted with astonishing realism, are making waves in the fashion and marketing industries. Unlike human influencers, they can be designed to fit any brand image, appear in multiple places simultaneously, and engage tirelessly with audiences. This ability to adapt instantly to the latest trends gives brands a powerful tool to shape public perception and influence fashion.

AI is also redefining our concepts of identity, both individually and collectively. Deepfake technology presents a new frontier where authenticity is questioned. By creating hyper realistic videos and images that can depict someone saying or doing things they never did, deepfakes blur the line between reality and fabrication. This raises profound questions about trust and authenticity in digital media. With AI-enhanced avatars in virtual reality spaces, individuals can explore identities beyond the limitations of the physical world. These avatars offer a platform for expression and creativity, allowing users to craft personas that reflect their aspirations, regardless of their real-world constraints. However, this fluidity in identity also challenges traditional notions of *self*—prompting us to reconsider what it means to be "real" in a virtual age.

There are also concerns about cultural homogenization. AI algorithms often recommend content based on popular trends, which can lead to a narrowing of the cultural spectrum. As platforms push content that aligns with user preferences, they may inadvertently limit exposure to diverse ideas and traditions. This algorithmic bias risks creating echo chambers, where individuals receive information that reinforces existing beliefs, reducing the richness of cultural diversity. In the globalized media landscape, there's a danger that local cultures might be overshadowed by dominant narratives, leading to a loss of unique cultural identities. As AI continues to influence content curation, it's important to ensure that diverse perspectives remain visible and accessible.

Yet, AI also offers remarkable opportunities for cultural preservation. Digital archiving technologies can document endangered languages, capturing their nuances and ensuring they are not lost to time. By transcribing spoken words and recording cultural practices, AI helps safeguard linguistic heritage for future generations. Virtual reality experiences can bring historical sites to life, offering immersive journeys through places that might be inaccessible or fragile. These experiences provide educational and cultural enrichment, allowing people worldwide to engage with history in a deeply personal way. By harnessing AI's capabilities, we can promote and preserve cultural heritage, ensuring that the past remains a vibrant part of our present and future.

Bridging the Digital Divide with AI

Imagine a small farm in a developing country, where traditional methods have long dictated the rhythm of planting and harvesting. Enter AI, with its potential to transform agriculture by improving crop yields. Farmers now have access to AI-powered tools that analyze soil conditions and weather patterns, offering real-time insights into the best planting times and crop rotations. This isn't just about increasing output; it's about doing so sustainably, reducing waste and improving food security. AI technologies help farmers make informed decisions, optimizing resource use and enhancing productivity. In regions where every grain counts, such advancements can make a profound difference, potentially lifting entire communities out of poverty.

Healthcare in remote areas faces its own set of challenges, but AI is stepping up with solutions that bridge the gap. AI-powered healthcare tools can offer diagnostic support, analyzing medical data to detect diseases early. For example, AI systems can scan images for signs of tuberculosis or diabetic retinopathy, conditions that might otherwise go unnoticed until it's too late. These technologies allow healthcare workers in remote regions to provide timely and accurate care, even without specialists on hand. AI also facilitates telemedicine, connecting patients with doctors miles away, ensuring that distance is no longer a barrier to receiving quality healthcare. In places where access to medical services is limited, AI becomes a lifeline, improving outcomes and saving lives.

But ensuring that AI benefits everyone requires strategic efforts to promote equitable access. Open-source AI platforms present one viable path, allowing innovators in less privileged areas to develop solutions tailored to their unique needs. By making AI tools and resources freely available, we democratize the ability to innovate, encouraging diverse solutions that address local challenges. International collaborations for technology transfer further amplify these efforts, fostering an exchange of knowledge and expertise across borders. These partnerships can help bridge gaps, ensuring that AI advancements do not remain the privilege of a few but become a shared resource for global good.

There are already promising examples of AI projects successfully reducing disparities. Consider AI literacy programs in underserved communities, which equip individuals with the skills to engage with and benefit from AI technologies. These programs focus on education and empowerment, teaching participants to use AI tools effectively and fostering a sense of agency in the digital world. Low-cost AI solutions for basic infrastructure needs also demonstrate how technology can be leveraged for impact. From solar-powered AI systems that monitor water quality to affordable AI-driven energy solutions, these innovations address fundamental needs, improving quality of life in tangible ways.

Yet, the path to widespread AI adoption is not without obstacles. Infrastructure limitations in rural areas pose significant challenges, as many regions still lack the basic connectivity needed to support AI technologies. Without reliable internet access, the potential for AI to drive development remains untapped. Additionally, cultural resistance to technological change can slow progress. In communities where traditional practices are deeply ingrained, introducing AI requires sensitivity and collaboration. It's essential to engage with local stakeholders, respecting cultural contexts and building trust to ensure AI is embraced as a partner in development rather than an intruder.

In examining AI's role in global development, it's clear that with the right strategies, AI can be a powerful tool for positive change. By addressing challenges and fostering inclusive access, we can unlock AI's potential to bridge the digital divide, creating opportunities for all.

12
THE AI COMMUNITY

P erhaps you'd like to be part of a group that shares your fascination with artificial intelligence—a place where every conversation spins new ideas and collaborations. That's the essence of engaging with the AI community. It's not just about absorbing information; it's about connecting with like-minded individuals who are just as curious and passionate about AI as you are. Whether you're a novice just dipping your toes into the AI pool or a seasoned expert looking to share your wisdom, there's a place for you.

One of the key starting points for anyone interested in AI is finding the right forums and communities. Consider Reddit's r/MachineLearning, a bustling hub with over a million members dedicated to discussing everything from the latest research papers to the quirks of machine learning models. The wealth of knowledge shared here is staggering, making it an invaluable resource for anyone keen to keep their finger on the pulse of AI advancements. For a more structured networking experience, LinkedIn offers numerous AI groups where professionals exchange insights, job opportunities, and emerging trends. These platforms provide a unique blend of casual interaction and professional networking, perfect for expanding your horizons.

Joining these communities has tangible benefits that go beyond simple knowledge exchange. Engaging with a diverse array of perspectives exposes you to different approaches to solving AI challenges, broadening your understanding and sparking your creativity. Collaborative projects often emerge from these interactions, leading to research partnerships or even startup ventures. Imagine brainstorming a novel AI application with someone halfway across the globe, each of you bringing unique insights that culminate in groundbreaking innovation. Such opportunities enhance your skill set and expand your professional network, opening doors to new career possibilities. Networking in these communities is an ongoing conversation, a way to stay sharp and inspired in a rapidly evolving field.

To make the most of these interactions, it's important to engage actively and authentically. Start by contributing to discussions. You don't have to be an expert to offer insights—often, simply asking the right questions can lead to enlightening discussions. Sharing resources, such as a recent article that may have caught your eye or a tool that has helped streamline your workflow, positions you as a valuable community member. Remember, feedback works both ways. Offering thoughtful feedback on others' posts not only helps them but also builds your reputation as a collaborative and engaged participant. In these communities, your voice matters, and the more you contribute, the more you stand to gain.

Networking isn't confined to the digital realm. Participating in AI conferences and meetups can significantly deepen your community engagement. These events offer face-to-face interaction, allowing you to connect with peers, mentors, and potential collaborators. Hackathons and coding competitions present another exciting avenue. They challenge you to apply your skills in real-world scenarios, often resulting in innovative solutions under tight timelines. These events foster a spirit of teamwork and problem-solving, reinforcing the idea that AI is as much about collaboration as it is about technology. The relationships forged in these settings often extend beyond the event, leading to lasting professional connections and friendships.

Contributing to Ethical AI Development

In a world where technology is advancing at a breakneck speed, the call for ethical AI becomes a conversation we all must engage in. If you've ever questioned how AI systems make their decisions or the fairness of those decisions, you're already on the path to advocating for ethical AI. Participating in public forums and debates about AI ethics is a good way to start. These platforms offer the opportunity to voice concerns, share insights, and even influence how AI is developed and deployed. Engaging in these discussions helps shape the future of AI and ensures that diverse voices contribute to a technology that affects us all. Supporting organizations dedicated to responsible AI development, such as *The Alan Turing Institute* or the *Center for Humane Technology*, can amplify your impact. These groups work to set standards and guidelines that prioritize transparency and fairness in AI systems. By aligning with them, you become part of a larger movement striving to make AI beneficial and equitable.

Open-source projects play a pivotal role in promoting transparency and collaboration in AI. By contributing to platforms like TensorFlow and PyTorch, you can help democratize access to AI tools and resources. Open-source communities thrive on the principle of shared knowledge, allowing anyone to contribute and benefit from collective advancements. Developing tools for bias detection and mitigation within these frameworks is particularly impactful. These contributions help address one of AI's most pressing challenges—ensuring that AI systems operate without perpetuating harmful biases. Open-source projects facilitate collaboration between developers, researchers, and enthusiasts, fostering an environment where innovation can flourish.

Policy discussions about AI ethics are another avenue where your voice can make a difference. Governments and organizations around the world are actively seeking input on how to regulate AI technologies. Submitting comments to government consultations on AI regulation allows you to shape policies that govern AI development and use. Engaging with AI ethics committees and think tanks provides a platform to discuss complex ethical issues and propose actionable solutions. These bodies often comprise experts from various fields who work together to craft guidelines that balance innovation with responsibility. Your participation in these discussions ensures that ethical considerations are integral to AI development, safeguarding both human rights and societal well-being.

Interdisciplinary collaboration is essential when addressing the ethical challenges posed by AI. Partnerships between technologists and ethicists are vital for integrating ethical principles into AI design and implementation. By working together, these experts can anticipate potential ethical dilemmas and devise strategies to mitigate them.

Collaborative research with social scientists can further enrich the ethical framework surrounding AI. Social scientists bring valuable insights into human behavior and societal impacts, helping to ensure that AI technologies are developed with a thorough understanding of their broader implications. This interdisciplinary approach fosters a holistic perspective on AI ethics, promoting solutions that are both innovative and socially responsible.

Reflection

Consider your interests and strengths. Reflect on how you can contribute to ethical AI development. Could you participate in discussions, contribute to open-source projects, engage with policymaking, or collaborate across disciplines? Identify one actionable step you can take today to advocate for ethical AI.

Staying Informed

One of the best ways to stay updated about the latest and greatest in AI is through online courses offered by platforms like Coursera and edX. These platforms provide a wide range of AI courses, from beginner-friendly introductions to advanced deep learning tutorials. Whether you're interested in machine learning algorithms or neural networks, these courses offer flexibility. You can learn at your own pace, fitting lessons into your schedule without the pressure of a traditional classroom setting. They're perfect for anyone looking to deepen their understanding while juggling other commitments.

Beyond courses, diving into AI literature can offer a more profound grasp of the field. This book, along with others, breaks down complex concepts into digestible insights, making it easier to understand how AI systems work and their potential impacts. Journals such as the *Journal of Artificial Intelligence Research* provide peer-reviewed articles that delve into the latest advancements and theories in AI. Reading these publications can keep you abreast of cutting-edge research and emerging trends, ensuring that your knowledge remains current and comprehensive.

For more immediate updates, subscribing to newsletters like *The AI Alignment Newsletter* can be helpful. These newsletters curate the latest news and developments in AI, delivering them straight to your inbox. They often include summaries of new research, interviews with leading AI experts, and discussions on the ethical implications of AI technologies. Following AI-focused news outlets is another effective way to stay informed. Outlets dedicated to AI provide continuous updates on technological advancements, policy changes, and industry shifts. This constant stream of information helps you remain aware of the rapid changes in the AI landscape, which can inform your personal and professional decisions.

The importance of lifelong learning cannot be overstated, especially in a field as dynamic as AI. A commitment to regular skill updates and certifications is mandatory. Technology evolves rapidly, and the skills in demand today might become obsolete tomorrow. By continually updating your knowledge, you ensure that you remain relevant and competitive in the job market. Participating in webinars and online workshops is an excellent way to keep learning. These sessions feature industry experts who share their insights and experiences, providing practical advice and strategies. They also offer opportunities for live interaction, allowing you to ask questions and engage in discussions with peers and professionals alike.

Future-Proofing Your Skills in an AI-Driven World

As the world becomes increasingly intertwined with artificial intelligence, the skills you develop today will shape your place in tomorrow's workforce. The AI era demands a blend of technical competencies and soft skills, making it imperative to align your expertise with these evolving needs. Technical skills such as programming and data analysis are the backbone of AI development. Whether you're writing code, analyzing datasets, or developing algorithms, these abilities are essential. They enable you to understand and create the systems that drive AI technologies. Learning languages like Python or R, which are widely used in data science and machine learning, can give you a significant edge. But the AI landscape is not just about hard skills; soft skills play an equally vital role. Critical thinking and adaptability ensure you can navigate complex problems and adjust to new advancements. These skills prepare you to respond to the unpredictable changes that come with technological evolution, making you a valuable asset in any field.

To stay ahead in this dynamic environment, you may want to enroll in specialized AI degree programs that offer structured learning paths, covering everything from foundational AI concepts to advanced machine learning techniques. These programs provide a comprehensive understanding of AI, equipping you with the knowledge needed to innovate and lead in this space. If formal education isn't your path, self-directed learning can be a flexible alternative. Online tutorials and resources are abundant, allowing you to learn at your own pace. Platforms like YouTube, GitHub, and online coding bootcamps offer lessons and projects that can enhance your skills without the constraints of traditional education. Engaging in real-world projects, even if they're small, can cement your learning and provide tangible results to showcase your growing expertise.

Adaptability is the cornerstone of thriving in an AI-driven world. The rapid pace of technological advancement means that new tools and technologies emerge regularly. Staying open to learning new programming languages or exploring interdisciplinary applications of AI is vital. For instance, combining AI skills with knowledge in fields like biology or finance can open new avenues for innovation and career opportunities. This adaptability not only keeps your skills sharp but also ensures you remain relevant as industries evolve. Embracing change and being willing to step outside your comfort zone allows you to seize opportunities that others might overlook, turning potential disruptions into advantages.

Proactive career planning is another critical element in preparing for the AI-infused future. Start by identifying emerging roles in AI and tech that align with your interests and strengths. Roles such as AI ethics consultant, machine learning engineer, or data scientist are increasingly in demand. Understanding these roles and the skills they require can help you tailor your learning efforts and career trajectory. Building a personal brand in the AI community is also important. Engage with professionals and share your insights through platforms like LinkedIn, blogs, or personal websites. This visibility can lead to new opportunities and collaborations, positioning you as a thought leader in your field. Networking with professionals and participating in industry events can further cement your presence in the AI community, opening doors to mentorship and career advancement.

The skills you cultivate and the strategies you employ will determine your ability to navigate and thrive in an AI-driven world.

Embracing continuous learning, adaptability, and proactive planning will ensure that you remain at the forefront of innovation. As you chart your path in this exciting landscape, remember that AI is not just reshaping industries—it's reshaping lives, offering endless possibilities for those ready to seize them.

CONCLUSION

W e have covered a lot of ground in this AI adventure, from unraveling the basics of AI to examining its transformative impact across various industries. We've tackled the ethical considerations that come with such powerful technology and looked at practical ways AI can be applied in our daily lives. Finally, we peered into the future, pondering AI's potential to reshape our world.

Throughout this book, we've seen that AI isn't just about machines taking over tasks. It's about enhancing what we can do and amplifying our abilities and recognizing the balance between the incredible opportunities AI offers and the challenges it presents. We've learned that AI can revolutionize industries, improve healthcare, and personalize education. But we've also discussed the importance of ethical development and the need to be vigilant about biases and privacy concerns.

AI is a double-edged sword. It can drive remarkable advancements, but it can also disrupt traditional ways of working and living. As you continue to engage with AI, remember to approach it with both optimism and caution—embrace its potential but remain aware of its implications. The future will be shaped by those who understand this balance.

Now, I urge you to act. Dive deeper into AI, whether it's through joining communities, taking courses, or experimenting with AI tools in your daily life (see the Resources Appendix that follows). These steps will enhance your understanding and position you to contribute meaningfully to the AI landscape. You have the power to be part of the conversation shaping AI's future.

Writing this book has been an eye-opening experience for me. Initially, I was skeptical about AI's role in writing. The idea of an algorithm potentially taking over my craft was daunting. But as I experimented with tools like ChatGPT for research and initial drafts, I realized AI is a collaborator, not a competitor. It assists in expanding ideas and exploring new angles, much like a writing partner. This journey deepened my appreciation for the synergy between human creativity and AI's computational capabilities.

The landscape of AI is continuously evolving. It's a field that promises to keep surprising us with its potential and challenges. I encourage you to remain curious and open to learning, as AI continues to advance and integrate more into our lives. There's an exciting future ahead, and staying informed will ensure you're ready to seize new opportunities. Back to the question I posed in the Introduction: *Is this thing going to steal my job?* The truthful answer is: *maybe*. But Artificial Intelligence can train you to get an even better job. And it will also increase your downtime, where you can potentially explore new hobbies—like learning more about AI. ;)

Thank you for sharing this journey with me. Your interest and engagement in understanding AI contributes to the collective exploration of this transformative technology. It's through our curiosity and efforts that we can shape a future where AI enhances our lives for the better.

As we move forward, let's hold on to a hopeful vision. AI has the potential to solve some of our most pressing challenges, from healthcare to environmental sustainability. It can enrich human life in ways we're only beginning to comprehend. Let's embrace these changes with optimism and proactive engagement. Together, we can navigate the complexities of AI and harness its power for the greater good.

Dear Reader,

I deeply grateful to you for reading my book. If you liked it, please leave review for on Amazon, which really helps independent authors promote their writing.

Gratefully,

Andrew Peterson

RESOURCES

This appendix serves as a starting point to explore the vast applications of AI across various domains. Each tool listed has been selected for its functionality, accessibility, and potential to improve efficiency or creativity in its respective area.

1. Education and Learning Tools

ChatGPT (OpenAI) • A conversational AI tool that assists in answering questions, tutoring, and generating content. Ideal for personalized learning and brainstorming.

Website: https://chat.openai.com

Pricing: Free tier available, Premium plans start at $20/month for GPT-4 access.

Example Use: Ask ChatGPT to help you summarize complex concepts from your coursework or generate practice questions for an upcoming exam.

Khan Academy (AI-powered Tutor) • An educational platform offering courses in a variety of subjects, with AI integrations like Khanmigo for personalized learning.

Website: https://www.khanacademy.org

Pricing: Free access; donations optional for additional support

Example Use: Use Khanmigo to receive step-by-step guidance in solving math problems or mastering coding basics.

Sora A platform connecting students to eBooks and audiobooks, with AI-driven recommendations for personalized reading lists.

Website: https://soraapp.com

Pricing: Free for schools with library partnerships.

Example Use: Build a customized reading list based on your interests or find book recommendations aligned with your coursework.

2. Language and Communication

Duolingo • An AI-powered language-learning app that uses gamification and adaptive learning for over 40 languages.

Website: https://www.duolingo.com

Pricing: Free; Duolingo Plus available at $12.99/month.

Example Use: Practice conversation skills with AI-driven exercises or reinforce vocabulary with gamified quizzes.

Grammarly • AI-driven writing assistant for grammar, style, and tone. Perfect for improving written communication.

Website: https://www.grammarly.com

Pricing: Free basic version; Premium plans start at $12/month.

Example Use: Edit your emails or polish a professional document to ensure clarity and accuracy.

DeepL • An AI translation service providing high-quality translations for multiple languages.

Website: https://www.deepl.com

Pricing: Free basic version; Pro plans start at $8.74/month.

Example Use: Translate complex legal or technical documents accurately to facilitate communication in a foreign language.

3. Creativity and Design

Canva (with AI Image Generator) • A versatile design platform offering templates for presentations, and marketing materials, with AI tools for generating images and enhancing designs.

Website: https://www.canva.com

Pricing: Free tier available; Pro plans start at $12.99/month.

Example Use: Design an eye-catching resume or create custom social media graphics effortlessly.

DALL·E (OpenAI) • An AI image generation tool for creating custom visuals from text prompts. Useful for marketing, education, and creative projects.

Website: https://openai.com/dall-e

Pricing: Pay-per-use credit system.

Example Use: Generate unique illustrations for a presentation or concept art for a creative project.

Runway ML •AI tools for video editing, image generation, and creative media projects, supporting workflows for filmmakers and designers.

Website: https://runwayml.com

Pricing: Free tier available; Pro plans start at $12/month.

Example Use: Edit videos with automated effects or create animated storyboards for your next project.

4. Career Coaching and Professional Growth

LinkedIn Learning • A platform for upskilling and career development, offering courses in AI, business, and technical skills.

Website: https://www.linkedin.com/learning

Pricing: Free trial; subscription starts at $39.99/month.

Example Use: Learn about AI applications in your industry or complete a course to earn a professional certification.

Eightfold.ai • An AI-driven career platform providing personalized job recommendations and career planning tools.

Website: https://www.eightfold.ai

Pricing: Custom pricing for enterprises.

Example Use: Discover new career opportunities tailored to your skills or receive guidance on crafting your career path.

Rezi • An AI-powered resume builder that optimizes content for applicant tracking systems.

Website: https://www.rezi.io

Pricing: Free basic version; Pro plans start at $29.95/year.

Example Use: Customize your resume for a specific job posting and ensure it meets ATS requirements.

5. Finance and Personal Organization

Mint • AI-enhanced personal finance management tool for budgeting, expense tracking, and financial planning.

Website: https://www.mint.com

Pricing: Free with optional premium services.

Example Use: Set up a budget with AI-guided recommendations or track spending habits to save more effectively.

YNAB (You Need A Budget) • An AI-integrated budgeting tool to help users take control of their finances.

Website: https://www.youneedabudget.com

Pricing: Free trial; $14.99/month or $99/year.

Example Use: Create a savings plan for a specific goal or analyze spending trends to cut unnecessary expenses.

Notion AI • An all-in-one workspace for organization and productivity, with AI tools for summarization, brainstorming, and task automation.

Website: https://www.notion.so

Pricing: Free for basic use; AI features in paid plans starting at $10/month.

Example Use: Draft project proposals or brainstorm ideas for your next big project.

6. Business and Productivity

Zapier • An AI-driven automation tool for connecting apps and automating workflows without coding.

Website: https://zapier.com

Pricing: Free for basic workflows; plans start at $19.99/month.

Example Use: Automate repetitive tasks, like sending follow-up emails or syncing calendar updates.

Slack (with AI integrations) • A collaboration platform with AI tools for summarizing conversations, automating tasks, and enhancing team productivity.

Website: https://slack.com

Pricing: Free tier available; Premium plans start at $7.25/user/month.

Example Use: Summarize lengthy team discussions to keep everyone aligned or automate status updates.

HubSpot (AI CRM tools) • A customer relationship management platform that uses AI to improve marketing, sales, and customer service.

Website: https://www.hubspot.com

Pricing: Free basic CRM; additional tools priced individually.

Example Use: Create targeted marketing campaigns or analyze customer data for actionable insights.

7. Miscellaneous Tools

Otter.ai • AI-powered transcription and meeting note-taking tool.

Website: https://otter.ai

Pricing: Free plan available; Premium plans start at $8.33/month.

Example Use: Automatically transcribe interviews or meetings for easier reference later.

Wolfram Alpha • An AI-powered computational engine for research, problem-solving, and knowledge discovery.

Website: https://www.wolframalpha.com

Pricing: Free; Pro plans start at $5.49/month.

Example Use: Solve complex equations or research data for academic or professional use.

IFTTT (If This Then That) • An AI automation platform for connecting apps and devices.

Website: https://ifttt.com

Pricing: Free tier available; Pro plans start at $2.50/month.

Example Use: Automate home devices to improve convenience, like turning lights off at a scheduled time.

GLOSSARY

Algorithm: A set of rules or instructions designed to solve a problem or perform a specific task, often executed by computers.

Artificial Intelligence (AI): The simulation of human intelligence processes by machines, including learning, reasoning, and self-correction.

Autonomous Vehicles: Vehicles equipped with AI systems to navigate and operate without human intervention, such as self-driving cars.

Bias in AI: Prejudices or systemic errors in AI systems, often caused by imbalanced or non-representative training data, leading to unfair outcomes.

Big Data: Extremely large and complex datasets that require advanced tools for processing and analysis, often used to train AI systems.

Chatbot: A conversational AI tool designed to simulate human-like interactions with users, often used in customer support or virtual assistance.

Data Mining: The process of analyzing large datasets to uncover patterns, trends, and useful information, often used to train AI models.

Deep Learning: A subset of machine learning involving neural networks with many layers, enabling systems to learn from vast amounts of data.

Explainable AI (XAI): AI systems designed to make their decision-making processes transparent and understandable to humans.

Generative AI: AI systems capable of creating new content, such as text, images, or music, by learning patterns from existing data.

Machine Learning (ML): A branch of AI focused on algorithms that learn from data and improve their performance over time without explicit programming.

Natural Language Processing (NLP): A field of AI focused on enabling machines to understand, interpret, and generate human language.

Neural Networks: Computational models inspired by the human brain, used to recognize patterns and process information in deep learning.

Predictive Analytics: The use of AI to analyze historical data and predict future outcomes, commonly applied in business and healthcare.

Reinforcement Learning: A type of machine learning where an AI system learns by interacting with its environment and receiving rewards or penalties.

Supervised Learning: A machine learning method where models are trained on labeled datasets to make predictions or classifications.

Turing Test: A measure of a machine's ability to exhibit human-like intelligence, based on its capacity to hold a conversation indistinguishable from a human.

Unsupervised Learning: A machine learning method where models learn patterns and structures in data without labeled outcomes.

Weak AI: AI systems designed for specific tasks, such as virtual assistants or recommendation systems, in contrast to general AI.

Zero-shot Learning: The ability of an AI system to make predictions or perform tasks it has not been explicitly trained for by generalizing from related knowledge.

REFERENCES

- AlphaGo. (n.d.). *DeepMind*. Retrieved from https://deepmind.google/research/breakthroughs/alphago/

- Artificial Intelligence (AI) coined at Dartmouth. (n.d.). Retrieved from https://home.dartmouth.edu/about/artificial-intelligence-ai-coined-dartmouth#:~:text=1956

- Artificial Intelligence in Risk Management. (n.d.). *KPMG*. Retrieved from https://kpmg.com/ae/en/home/insights/2021/09/artificial-intelligence-in-risk-management.html

- AI vs. Machine Learning vs. Deep Learning vs. Neural Networks. (n.d.). *IBM*. Retrieved from https://www.ibm.com/think/topics/ai-vs-machine-learning-vs-deep-learning-vs-neural-networks

- AI winter. (n.d.). *Wikipedia*. Retrieved from https://en.wikipedia.org/wiki/AI_winter

- Boost customer satisfaction with emotional AI intelligence in customer service. (n.d.). *Convin AI*. Retrieved from https://convin.ai/blog/center-experience-with-emotional-ai#:~:text=Emotional%20AI%20in%20Customer%20Service

- Breaking the echo: How AI shapes our digital echo chambers. (n.d.). *Propelland*. Retrieved from https://propelland.com/intelligence/how-ai-shapes-our-digital-echo-chambers/

- Deep Blue versus Garry Kasparov. (n.d.). *Wikipedia*. Retrieved from https://en.wikipedia.org/wiki/Deep_Blue_versus_Garry_Kasparov#:~:text=Deep%20Blue%20versus%20Garry%20Kasparov

- Deepfakes and identity theft. (n.d.). *PXL Vision*. Retrieved from https://www.pxl-vision.com/en/blog/deepfakes-and-identity-theft

- Ethics of artificial intelligence. (n.d.). *UNESCO*. Retrieved from https://www.unesco.org/en/artificial-intelligence/recommendation-ethics

- History of artificial intelligence. (n.d.). *Encyclopedia Britannica*. Retrieved from https://www.britannica.com/science/history-of-artificial-intelligence

- IBM's Watson was once heralded as the future of healthcare: What went wrong? (n.d.). *Healthcare Digital*. Retrieved from https://www.healthcare.digital/single-post/ibm-s-watson-was-once-heralded-as-the-future-of-healthcare-what-went-wrong#:~:text=Exec%20Summary

- How Amazon Alexa works using NLP. (n.d.). *Analytics Vidhya*. Retrieved from https://www.analyticsvidhya.com/blog/2024/08/how-amazon-alexa-works-using-nlp/

- How Khan Academy leveraged AI to change education. (n.d.). *Cut the SaaS*. Retrieved from https://www.cut-the-saas.com/ai/how-khan-academy-leveraged-ai-to-change-education

- How is AI improving access to healthcare in remote areas? (n.d.). *Express Healthcare*. Retrieved from https://www.expresshealthcare.in/blogs/guest-blogs-healthcare/how-is-ai-improving-access-to-healthcare-in-remote-areas-with-a-high-success-rate/444276/

- Jetson AGX Orin for next-gen robotics. (n.d.). *NVIDIA*. Retrieved from https://www.nvidia.com/en-us/autonomous-machines/embedded-systems/jetson-orin/

- Revolutionizing healthcare: The role of artificial intelligence. (2023). *BMC Medical Education*. Retrieved from https://bmcmededuc.biomedcentral.com/articles/10.1186/s12909-023-04698-z

- TensorFlow and its ecosystem: Artificial Intelligence (AI). (n.d.). *Medium*. Retrieved from https://medium.com/@AIandInsights/tensorflow-and-its-ecosystem-bfb26e7b09de

- Timeline of artificial intelligence. (n.d.). *Wikipedia*. Retrieved from https://en.wikipedia.org/wiki/Timeline_of_artificial_intelligence

- The impact of Big Data on AI advancements. (n.d.). *Data Center Dynamics*. Retrieved from https://www.datacenterdynamics.com/en/opinions/the-impact-of-big-data-on-ai-advancements/

- The 7 best data mining tools in 2025. (n.d.). *CareerFoundry*. Retrieved from https://careerfoundry.com/en/blog/data-analytics/best-data-mining-tools/

- The Amazon recommendations secret to selling more. (n.d.). *Rejoiner*. Retrieved from https://www.rejoiner.com/resources/amazon-recommendations-secret-selling-online

- The basics of neural networks: Explained using pizza analogy. (n.d.). *Medium*. Retrieved from https://medium.com/@kirtankarvaibhav24/the-basics-of-neural-networks-explained-using-pizza-analogy-f685da3d3abb

- The future of AI in music and fine art: A creative revolution. (n.d.). *ArtPlug*. Retrieved from https://artplug.com/ai-in-music-and-fine-art/

- The state of AI in 2023: Generative AI's breakout year. (2023). *McKinsey & Company*. Retrieved from https://www.mckinsey.com/~/media/mckinsey/business%20functions/quantumblack/our%20insights/the%20state%20of%20ai%20in%202023%20generative%20ais%20breakout%20year/the-state-of-ai-in-2023-generative-ais-breakout-year_vf.pdf

- Top 25 artificial intelligence and Big Data news publications. (n.d.). *Certainly*. Retrieved from https://certainly.io/blog/top-ai-big-data-publications/

- Top AI communities in 2023. (n.d.). *Medium*. Retrieved from https://medium.com/ai-vanguard/top-ai-communities-in-2023-403254cb05f1

- We tested 50+ AI productivity tools. Here are the 16 best. (n.d.). *UseMotion*. Retrieved from https://www.usemotion.com/blog/ai-productivity-tools

- What is a neural network? (n.d.). *IBM*. Retrieved from https://www.ibm.com/think/topics/neural-networks

- How to future-proof your career: Surviving in the AI era. (2024). *Forbes*. Retrieved from https://www.forbes.com/sites/davidhenkin/2024/05/09/how-to-future-proof-your-career-surviving-in-the-ai-era/

www.ingramcontent.com/pod-product-compliance
Lightning Source LLC
Chambersburg PA
CBHW070932210326
41520CB00021B/6906